# Easy ways to CHRISTMAS PLAYS

# Easy ways to CHRISTMAS PLAYS

## Vicki Howie

**Published by The Bible Reading Fellowship**
First Floor, Elsfield Hall
15—17 Elsfield Way, Oxford OX2 8FG
ISBN 1 84101 017 0
ISBN-13 978 1 84101 017 5

First edition 1998
10 9 8 7 6 5 4 3 2

A catalogue record for this book
is available from the British Library

Printed in Great Britain by Lightning Source

# CONTENTS

# Introduction

Christmas seemed such a long way off when you cheerfully agreed to put on a nativity play with your lively group of 3–7 year olds! Now, however, the play day is firmly in your church or school diary and fast approaching. Plans must be made! But where will you find a script that tells the familiar Christmas story in a new and exciting way and yet is easy enough for even the youngest child in your group? How will you produce an effective play in the short time available in a way that all the children (and the audience) will thoroughly enjoy? How will you manage to keep the attention of the three year olds? And how will you encourage the older ones to speak up and move confidently around the stage or hall?

This book, containing three simple plays, each with its own five-week countdown to the play day, is designed to show you how!

## The plays

Each of the three plays, which have all been performed successfully by a Sunday school group of mixed ages and abilities, explores a different Christian theme and takes approximately twenty minutes to perform.

*Come to a party!* is the simplest play, and reminds the children that Christmas is Jesus' birthday. Most children love birthday parties, and the activities that lead to the play include party games, simple crafts with party cups and straws, and group discussions about balloons, jelly and birthday cake!

*The star who couldn't twinkle* is about a little star whose light fades away because he is too shy to make friends with God. Only baby Jesus can help him come closer to God and start to sparkle. Once again, the activities relate to the theme, helping the children to understand what their nativity play is all about.

*Shine your lights!* is the most challenging of the three plays and would suit a group of children at the top end of the age range, many of whom would like a line to say or a special part to play. It is set in a village in Victorian times and features a group of carol singers who discover the real meaning of Christmas one snowy Christmas Eve.

No two groups of children will be the same and so ideas are given in the introduction to each play on how to adapt it to suit your particular group—perhaps reducing the number of speaking parts for a younger group, or adding more for an older group. Flexibility is the word!

Generally speaking, all the children remain on the stage (or stage area) throughout the play, to do away with any complicated entries and exits and to allow them to see the entire play instead of waiting off-stage for their special moment. Everyone is kept interested and involved during the play with lots of mimes, actions and songs.

Clues are written into the narrative to help the children remember when to say their line, move across the stage, sit down or stand up and also to help you remember what everyone should be doing. Some simple plans show you where the children stand at the start, middle and end of the play.

## Countdown to the play day!

Can you remember your first appearance in a nativity play? Did you find yourself inexplicably dressed in strange clothes for a performance which you experienced in a terrified daze? Were you ready for the sea of faces that came to watch you? Afterwards, did you know what the whole thing was all about? Probably not!

The countdown to the play day was written with this in mind. It provides a complete learning experience for the children in your group, the play being the natural climax. It includes introductory talks with suggested visual aids, an illustrated story of the play, graded activity sheets, tips for each rehearsal and closing prayers all designed to help the children understand:

- at five weeks to go—the **theme** of the play
- at four weeks to go—the **characters** in the play (to include help with casting the parts)
- at three weeks to go—the **actions, mimes and movements** in the play (often practised in party-type games)
- at two weeks to go—the **costumes and props** (which are kept very simple)
- at one week to go—what will happen on the **play day**

One final section, *It's the play day!* gives some practical hints on preparing for the performance and on helping the children to feel happy and confident about their play.

Throughout, the emphasis is on learning through play rather than drilling the children to provide a polished performance. Only a few essential props are required and the children are encouraged to look for simple costumes at home.

## The activity sheets

The photocopiable activity sheets are designed to back up the teaching elements in each weekly session. It is up to you to choose which activities you would like your group to do. Only you will know what the children in your group can manage and enjoy, but as a guide the sheets are marked

- with a **robin** for 3 year olds
- with a **snowflake** for 4–5 year olds
- with a **Christmas cracker** for 6–7 year olds

Suggestions are given in the text on the best way to make use of these sheets.

**The activity sheets in the 'Four weeks to go' section contain the lines spoken by the children in the play, with helpful illustrations. Give them to the children to use in rehearsals and to take home for extra practice.**

Those in the 'Three weeks to go' section can be used to tell parents which character their child will be in the play, and contain ideas on finding a simple costume at home.

The poster in the 'One week to go' section can be used to advertise the play and to inform parents of the date, time and place of the play.

## Craft items

All the craft ideas in this book are very simple. It is assumed that pencils, crayons, scissors (for the older ones) and glue are available for the children to use. If any other craft material is required, advance warning is given in the 'Memos for next week' paragraph at the end of each weekly session. These additional items involve easy-to-find materials such as foil, paper plates or thin card.

The 'Memos for next week' remind you of everything you will need for the next session, including any cutting out for the youngest children. Don't forget to save time by cutting out a pile of sheets in one go!

## Songs and carols

Several new easy-to-learn songs, set to familiar tunes, are included in the play scripts. Elsewhere, appropriate carols and songs are suggested, or you may like to use your own favourites at these points. The less traditional carols suggested can be found in *Carol, gaily carol* published by A & C Black, with the exception of 'A starry night' which can be found in *Merrily to Bethlehem*, also published by A & C Black, or *Chester's Easiest Christmas Music* published by Chester Music Limited.

Practise your chosen songs and carols each week so that the children are familiar with them by the play day. Often just one verse will suffice, otherwise the play will go on for too long.

## Where to begin

Read through the introduction to each play (which precedes the countdown) and the play scripts. Decide which play would best suit your group, remembering that you can always adapt it. Decide which songs to sing and write these on the script. From there on, follow the countdown to the play day, referring to the 'Memos for next week' in order to have everything ready for the next session.

Don't forget that some children may not come from the 'perfect' family unit, or may not have a mum or dad coming to see them in the play. Bear this in mind and choose your words carefully, especially when talking to the children about the play day.

Give lots of praise ... have fun ... and enjoy these *Easy Ways to Christmas Plays!*

# Come to a
# PARTY!

# INTRODUCTION

*If you've just accepted an invitation to perform this nativity play in a few weeks' time, then welcome to the party!*

*The theme of the play is that Christmas is really a big birthday party to celebrate the birth of Jesus, and you will find that the story, activities and the play itself are written in 'birthday' language.*

*Before you start working with the children, read through all the material and familiarize yourself with the play. Give copies of the play to your helpers so that they will know how to help the children at the very first rehearsal.*

## Adapting the play to suit your group

*Come to a party!* was written specifically for a group of 3–7 year olds with only a short time to rehearse each week. It was designed to give the older ones a chance to say a line, while keeping the younger ones interested and involved throughout in actions and mimes.

However, if your group consists mainly of younger children, the play can be simplified further by reducing the number of innkeepers and glowing angels, or further still by integrating any or all of the speaking parts into the narration and simply letting the children mime the story.

Conversely, you could add more speaking parts with an older group, by giving lines to Mary and Joseph, the shepherds and kings, and by using more than one narrator. Look at the story 'A party for baby Jesus' on pages 11–14 for some ideas.

## Casting

At this stage, it is helpful to have some idea about who will play the main parts, so you may like to pencil in some possible names beside the list of main characters below. (The activities in the 'Four weeks to go' section of the count-down, on pages 15–16, will help you to make a final choice, and you can then divide the rest of the children into three groups of shepherds, angels and kings.)

### Main characters

*The narrator*—a leader or helper if your group consists of young children
*Mary and Joseph*—two enthusiastic children who can react well to the other children, but who don't need to speak any lines
*The angel Gabriel*—someone with a strong voice who could also be the leader of all the younger angels
*Two grumpy innkeepers and one kind innkeeper*—three children who would enjoy character parts!
*Two glowing angels*

The remaining children are shepherds, angels or kings.

(Note that the lines written in the play for the main characters are suggestions only, as the activities will encourage the children to make up their own words.)

## Essential props

Four chairs or stools
Three cushions (one for each innkeeper)
A box or basket for the manger
A baby doll to represent Jesus
A big shiny star

## After the performance

You may like to continue the party theme by asking the audience to stay on after the play for refreshments. This would be a good opportunity to reward the children for all their hard work and allow parents to get to know each other. Why not hang up some bunches of balloons and use birthday serviettes, paper cups and straws?

## Memos for next week

• Read 'Five weeks to go'
• Take along a balloon to blow up
• Photocopy the activity sheets you want to use, and cut out the missing pictures for Jesus' birthday card ready for the youngest children

Depending on your choice of activities, you may need:
• an old microphone (or improvise with a cardboard roll)
• old Christmas and birthday cards, a hole-puncher and some thin ribbon
• old Christmas and birthday cards cut in half in a zig-zag fashion for the jigsaw game

# 5 4 3 2 1

## Five weeks to go – Introducing the theme of the play

This week, the aim is to tell the children the Christmas story and to explain that Christmas is Jesus' birthday.

Ask the children to sit down quietly because you're going to tell them a story all about a birthday party.

Encourage them to start thinking about birthdays by saying, *Hands up if you like birth-days! … Did you have a birthday party, Peter? … Was it fun? … Did you blow up any bal-loons? …* (Make everyone laugh with your attempts to blow up the balloon and ask them to blow when you blow! If you manage to inflate it, release it and let it whizz round the room!) … *What about you, Emma, did you eat ice-cream and jelly? …* (Get everyone to mime eating and say 'Mmm') … *Hands up if you blew out all the candles on your cake? … Can you show me how hard you can blow? Wait for it! One, two, three, BLOW!*

Explain that Christmas is Jesus' birthday party and that you are going to tell them what happened at the very first Christmas when Jesus was born.

Read '*A party for baby Jesus*', making sure that the children see all the pictures at the appropriate moments.

# A party for baby Jesus

This is the story of a very unusual birthday party. It didn't happen in a warm house with jelly and cake on the table, but in a chilly stable with horses and sheep and a manger full of hay. And there were no colourful balloons tied to the gatepost, but instead a big shiny star hung in the sky!

Angels held the party to welcome a very special baby into the world. This is how it happened.

Long ago, God wanted to say how much he loved us. He decided to send us a wonderful present. It was the best Christmas present anyone ever had. It was a baby boy—God's very own son.

God knew that the baby would need a kind mother and father to look after him in this world, so he sent his messenger, the angel Gabriel, to speak to Mary. She was soon to marry a carpenter called Joseph.

'Don't be afraid, Mary,' said the angel. 'God loves you so much that he wants you to have a very special baby. He will be God's own son and you must call him Jesus.'

Mary gasped. 'To think that God should choose me! I will do whatever he asks!'

Mary was very busy getting everything ready for the baby. She grew rounder as the baby grew bigger, and she needed lots of rest. But just when the baby was nearly ready to be born, Mary and Joseph had to walk all the way to Bethlehem to sign their names on a register.

'Is it much further?' asked Mary. 'I'm worn out and I think the baby is about to be born!'

'Don't worry, we're nearly there,' said Joseph.

He put his arm around Mary and helped her along the rough road. But when he saw the busy town, Joseph began to worry. Bethlehem was positively buzzing with

people—it was bursting at the seams. If only he could find a room for Mary to rest.

They knocked on lots of doors. Rat-a-tat-tat. Rat-a-tat-tat. But the innkeepers were fed up with answering the door and said, 'No room,' or 'Can't you read the "full" sign?' in grumpy voices.

At last, a very kind innkeeper said, 'You both look so tired. Would you like to stay the night in my stable? Don't mind the animals!'

That night, stars glowed like birthday candles in the night sky. And that night, God sent us that wonderful present—his son, the baby Jesus.

'I think you want to go to sleep,' said Mary, wrapping the baby in cloths and giving him a cuddle. 'Let's see if you'd be happy in the manger!'

A huge crowd of excited angels played

'Follow my leader' all the way to the stable roof. They wanted to give a party for baby Jesus.

'Can you give us an extra twinkle?' they asked a big star. 'Then people will know the party is here!'

'But who can we invite?' asked a glowing angel. 'Everyone's asleep!'

'Everyone except those shepherds,' said another glowing angel. 'Shall we fly down with a party invitation?'

The shepherds were terrified when the angels appeared, sparkling like party fireworks! They covered their eyes with their hands.

'Dear shepherds, don't be afraid,' said the angels. 'Please come to a birthday party in Bethlehem. It's for baby Jesus.

You'll find him wrapped in cloths and lying in a manger.'

'We'd love to come!' replied the shepherds. They gathered up some lambs to take to the baby and hurried down the hill into Bethlehem.

Far away in the east, three kings saw the birthday star.

'Someone special must be having a party!' they said. 'Let's take precious gifts of gold, frankincense and myrrh, and find out who it is. We can follow the star.'

What a wonderful time they all had in that stable, talking and laughing and opening the presents... but most of all, admiring baby Jesus. Mary gazed around her, trying to remember everything, for she knew that such an unusual birthday party, with angels, shepherds and kings, would never ever happen again.

# Activity time

Divide the children into groups according to which activity sheet you want them to do. The Christmas Cracker sheet (pages 23–24) is for the older children, with the middle and youngest groups (Snowflakes and Robins) making the birthday card for Jesus (pages 25–26).

## The Christmas Crackers

### Birthday survey

With your microphone at the ready, interview some of the more confident children about their birthdays, using the questions on the clipboard as a starter, but developing the interviews to find out how each person celebrated their last birthday or would like to celebrate the next. Ask all the children to fill in the survey sheet (giving help where necessary) and to look for the clue about Jesus' birthday.

### What's alike?

Look at Sam's two photographs with the children and talk about the two parties. Ask them to find the five things in common (pointing out that this is the opposite of a 'spot the difference' puzzle): *the cake, the cards, the candles, the presents and friends.* Encourage *all* their suggestions, just saying, *Well, does a cat help us to celebrate Christmas? Not really. What else can you find?* when they pick out any red herrings! Give clues if necessary.

## Snowflakes and Robins

Both groups can make and colour a birthday card for Jesus. (Make sure you have the cutting out done ready for the younger ones.) If you are short of time, leave out the cake and balloons meant for the inside of the card.

Show the front of the card (page 26) to the children and use the words on it to remind them of the Christmas story. For example, say, *At Christmas, Mary and Joseph came to Bethlehem. At Christmas, Jesus was born in a stable. Mary had to put him in the manger. In a minute we'll glue the picture of Jesus on to the card. At Christmas, the shepherds came to see Jesus and they brought him a present. Can you remember what that was? ... etc.*

When the cards are complete, ask the children to colour them in and write their own names on the inside.

## Further ideas

**Play the jigsaw game.** Scatter the jigsaw pieces of old birthday and Christmas cards (see page 10) on the floor and see who can collect the most complete cards, either individually or in teams.

**Make tags for Christmas and birthday presents.** Suggestions are shown on the Christmas Cracker sheet (page 24).

## Closing prayer

*Thank you, God, for all the fun we have at birthdays.*
*Thank you for balloons to blow up,*
    *and candles to blow out.*
*Thank you for friends to play with,*
    *and presents to open.*
*But most of all, thank you for baby Jesus*
    *who was born at Christmas.*
*Help us to remember that Christmas is Jesus' birthday.*
*Amen*

## Memos for next week

• Read 'Four weeks to go'
• Read the play again and study the 'starting position' for all the children
• Make sure you have the essential props ready to use straight away. (Try to set up the stage before the children arrive.)
• If possible, take a music stand to put the play on when you are directing the action
• Take the figures from a nativity set, if you have any

- If you are intending to make the paper-cup characters, you will need paper cups, glue or sticky tape (and pipe cleaners if you wish). Try to make one of each in advance, if you have time. Do any necessary cutting out for the youngest ones

## Four weeks to go - Introducing the characters

The aim this week is to encourage the children to think about the people in the nativity story: what they did, how they felt and what they might have said. The activities will help everyone to decide who they would like to be in the play and, in the case of the main characters, what they are going to say.

Ask the children about their favourite stories or pantomimes.

For example, ask, *Do you like the story of Little Red Riding Hood? ... Who did she go to visit? ... Can you remember what animal she met on the way? ... Do you think she was frightened? ... I wonder what she said to the wolf? ...* etc.

Remind the children about the story you told them last week of the very first Christmas. Emphasize that this is a true story and that you can read about it in the Bible.

Ask them if they can remember any of the people in the story. As they give the various names, briefly describe that person's role. For example, *That's right, the angel Gabriel. He was the one who told Mary she was going to have a baby called Jesus ... Yes, Joseph. He took Mary on the long journey to Bethlehem...* etc.

Show the pictures from the story again as you do this, or use the figures from a nativity set.

## Activity time

### The Christmas Crackers

Give the Christmas Cracker sheet (pages 27 and 28) to those children you think will be playing the main parts. Talk about the various situations, pointing out the expressions on the characters' faces and discussing how they must have felt. Then ask them to have a go at filling in the speech bubbles and the invitation. (Remind them about the 'helpful words' on each page.)

Ask the children to read out their ideas to the group and give lots of praise.

Decide yourself who is going to play each part, basing your decision on your knowledge of the children and on their responses to the activity sheet. (Don't force anyone to have a speaking part if they are too shy. Instead, you could make them feel important by asking if they'd like to be a chief shepherd, angel or king with responsibility for helping the younger ones, or the angel who gives baby Jesus to Mary.) However, the innkeepers could discuss between themselves who are going to be the grumpy ones, and who is going to be the very kind one who lends his stable to Mary and Joseph.

Write down the final decision for future reference and make sure everyone knows exactly who he or she is going to be. Give everyone an activity sheet to take home so that they can think again about what they are going to say in the play. They will find it easier to say their own words, rather than trying to remember set lines.

You may like to give the Snowflake sheet to anyone who has decided to be a chief shepherd, angel or king, or who simply wants to act with the younger ones.

### Snowflakes

This activity sheet (page 29) is designed to encourage the children to think about what the shepherds, angels and kings did in the Christmas story and then to decide who they'd like to be.

It's a good idea to read out the party invitation and reply, asking for spoken answers before getting everyone to write in the missing words. Point out that the answers can all be found on the page.

When the children have coloured in the balloons and the star in 'Where is the party?'

*Rat-a-tat-tat!*

and 'Where is baby Jesus?' (page 30) they can draw themselves in the picture frame, in costume if they wish.

Make a note of who each child wants to be, for future reference.

## Robins

Show the children the angel, shepherd and king paper-cup characters if you have managed to make any in advance. Briefly remind them of their roles in the Christmas story.

Ask each child what they would like to be in the story and give them the appropriate face and accessory to colour in. Help them with the gluing or sticking, pointing out that they are using party cups because Christmas is Jesus' birthday.

(You can add a pipe-cleaner crook to the shepherd for the more dextrous.)

Make a note of who the children want to be, for future reference, and let them take their puppets to the first rehearsal. You can then see at a glance what character each child is in the play and so where they should stand.

## It's play time!

Put the chairs, cushions and manger in position if you haven't already done so. (See stage plan on page 35.) Hide the star and baby doll behind the two chairs in the stable area.

Take each group of kings, angels and shepherds to stand in the appropriate place, and then ask Mary and Joseph and the innkeepers to sit on their chairs and cushions. (Don't panic if all this takes time; it's quite normal for it to be a noisy and confusing episode!) Refer to your notes if anyone has forgotten who they are supposed to be.

If possible, have an adult helper with each group. Identify your chief shepherd, angel and king and remind them to help the little ones.

Ask everyone to watch you and to copy what you do. Then, as the narrator starts to read the play, lead the children in the mimes. Smile, give lots of encouragement, and act as you

would if you were getting everyone to play an enjoyable party game.

As yet, the children will be hesitant when given any instructions to move around the stage, so step forward, take a hand and walk with them. (The activities for next week will help to build their confidence.)

Make sure that your narrator pauses long enough to allow for the mimes or other actions, but also keeps the story going fairly briskly. The children will lose interest if there are long gaps.

Sing any carols the children already know at the appropriate moments. Otherwise, say *This is where we'll sing... which we're going to learn later on.*

If you don't have time for the whole play (and you probably won't!), remind the children of the way the story ends and get each group to practise coming to the manger. Make a note to start next week where you left off.

## Closing prayer

*Thank you, God, for helping us with our Christmas play today.*
*Sometimes, Christmas seems such a long way away and we can't wait to get there.*
*Help us to be just as patient as Mary and Joseph were on that long walk to Bethlehem, when they were waiting for baby Jesus to be born.*
**Amen**

## Memos for next week

• Read 'Three weeks to go'

For *Pass the Parcel* you will need:

• a tape of carols or nursery rhymes or someone to play the carols on the piano. This will help the children to learn the tunes and they might even sing along!
• a small present wrapped in about eight layers
• the forfeits, cut up and placed in an envelope

For *Simon Says* you will need the list of actions on the activity sheet (page 32).

Music is also needed for *Musical Cushions* and *Follow my Leader*.

## Three weeks to go - Let's play party games

This week, the children stay in one group to play party games designed to help them act their parts and move confidently around the stage in the play.

Say, *As Christmas is Jesus' birthday, we're all going to play some party games. Everyone sit in a circle, please, for Pass the Parcel.*

### Pass the Parcel

Put baby Jesus in the manger in the middle of the circle with the forfeits in an envelope at his feet (see activity sheet, page 32.)

Explain that this is Pass the Parcel with a difference. When the music stops, the person holding the parcel must take off a layer, go to admire the baby in the manger and then hand you a forfeit from the envelope. (It doesn't matter which one.)

Read out the forfeit, which will contain an acting job for one or more of the characters in the play. When the appropriate child has done the forfeit and everyone has applauded, the game can continue.

When all the forfeits have gone, carry on with the traditional game until the present is unwrapped.

Remember that this is a good opportunity to encourage the children to act and speak out. Say, for example, *Did everyone hear that? I'm sure you could say that a bit louder! Have another go!*

Everyone can sing *Here we go up to Bethlehem* (or your chosen carol) when Joseph takes Mary on the long journey.

Give the forfeits to the appropriate children at the end of the game.

### Simon Says

Ask your narrator to call out the instructions from the *Simon Says* list on the activity sheet (page 32), in any order.

Either play the traditional game, where the children should only follow an instruction if prefixed with the words 'Simon says', *or* ask the children to do everything just for fun. In the former case, those who are 'out' sit down, and the last one left standing is the winner.

### Musical Cushions

Everyone sits in a circle, with the three innkeepers on their cushions in the centre. When the music plays, they must walk in a big circle around the three cushions. When the music stops, they must dash to sit on any cushion. After a practice run, take one cushion away in the traditional way. The innkeeper left without a cushion next time the music stops is out. Carry on to find out who is the winner.

Remind the innkeepers that they will *sit* on their cushions at the start of the play, *stand up* to answer the door to Mary and Joseph, and *sit down* again afterwards.

### Follow my Leader

Seat everyone in a circle again, with the three cushions spread out in the middle and the manger a little way outside the circle. Ask the chief shepherd to stand up and the other shepherds to make a line behind him. Then say, *Let's play Follow my Leader. Ben, lead your shepherds in and out of the cushions, any way you like, and then take them to kneel at the manger.*

Play music while they do this, and if they carry on for too long, say, *Lovely, now off you go to the manger—whichever way you like!*

## It's play time!

If you stopped halfway through the play last week, quickly talk and walk the children up to that point before starting in earnest where you left off. Otherwise, the shepherds and kings may feel they never get to their bit! Even so, practise the mimes at the beginning, and practise chanting *Rat-a-tat-tat*.

Give lots of praise and don't worry if the children seem to have forgotten everything from last week. It's still early days and the important thing is to make it all good fun.

## Closing prayer

*Father God, we thank you for all the happy times we have playing games with our friends.*
*We praise you that a great king like Jesus was born for us in a simple stable and came to be our friend.*
*Amen*

# COUNTDOWN TO THE PLAY DAY!

## Memos for next week

- Read 'Two weeks to go'
- Take along any pictures you can find of biblical costumes
- Photocopy the activity sheet on dressing up from page 33.

For the *paper crowns,* you will need:
- paper-crown shapes, stickers, glitter and tinsel for decoration, and sticky tape or staples for fastening

For the *precious gifts,* you will need:
- small boxes and wrapping paper or foil

For the *dressing-up game,* you will need:
- the dressing-up clothes, a toy sheep, music to play and a small present in an envelope

## Two weeks to go - costumes and props

Leave more time this week for practising the play.

Warn parents (perhaps via the activity sheet) that you'd like the children to come dressed in an appropriate, *simple* costume on the day of the play.

Introduce the subject of costumes. Say, *Put up your hand if you've ever been to a fancy dress party … What did you go as, Radhika? … What did you wear?*

Show the children any pictures you have found in nativity books or old Christmas cards (or use the pictures in '*A party for baby Jesus*') of the different characters. Talk about what they are wearing. Ask, *Who's going to be a shepherd in our play? … What do you think you could dress up in? … Yes! A dressing gown would be good … or a big stripey T-shirt, yes! …* etc. Repeat this process with the other characters and make sure that Mary in particular has something suitable to wear or can borrow something.

## Activity time

Keep this fairly short today to leave lots of time for the play.

The activity sheet should encourage everyone to look for dressing-up clothes at home.

## Further ideas

### Paper crowns

Help the children to decorate paper crowns with crayons, stickers, glitter, and tinsel glued around the base. Measure around the children's heads and staple or tape the paper into place at the right size.

### Precious gifts

The children can make gifts for the kings to offer by wrapping small boxes (such as variety-pack cereal boxes) in foil or wrapping paper.

### Dressing-up game

Everyone sits in a circle. Place a boy's dressing-gown, a tea-towel, a head-band and a toy sheep on the floor in the middle.

When the music starts, the children pass round an envelope containing a small present, such as a bookmark. Whoever is holding the envelope when the music stops must try to dress up as a shepherd before the music starts again. (You will need to give some help.) Allow too little time for each child to finish dressing up until you want the game to finish. At the end of the game the shepherd can keep the present.

### It's play time!

Try to go through the entire play this week, singing all the carols at the appropriate moments. It's important that the children see the play as a complete story now, rather than in confusing bits and pieces.

Call out *Follow my leader* to remind them to walk in a confident and orderly way to the stable.

Try to make the rehearsal as much fun as possible. If you are tense, this will communicate itself to the children. Remember that the teaching aspects of this play are far more important than giving a polished performance.

## closing prayer

*Thank you, Lord Jesus, for all the fun of dressing up*
*and pretending to be shepherds, angels and kings.*
*Thank you that we can come to your birthday party*
*just as we are, because you love us so much.*
***Amen***

## Memos for next week

- Read 'One week to go'
- Photocopy the poster and complete the 'Please bring…' section for the youngest children
- Make sure that all your arrangements are in place for the day of the play, including any plans you have for refreshments afterwards

## One week to go —

## come to our play!

This week, be determined to leave as much time as you need to rehearse the play without letting other activities overrun.

Talk to the children about the play day. Ask them who they are going to invite. Explain that the visitors want to hear the story about the very first Christmas and that's why you are going to act it out for them.

Ask everyone what he or she has found to wear in the play, as a reminder to any who may have forgotten to look. Some children may say they couldn't find anything to wear, so make a note to speak to their parents to see if you can help. Find out if anyone can bring a toy sheep or lamb.

Ask all the children to colour in the poster advertising the play. The older children can fill in the 'Please bring…' section at the bottom. Use this as appropriate, for example, …*cakes or biscuits, friends and relatives*, or simply, *Emma dressed in her costume!*

## It's play time!

Get everyone to line up in the right order, ready to file on to the stage area. (You will find the order at the beginning of the play on page 21.)

Practise walking quietly on to the stage and into the starting position. Note that everyone should remain standing to begin the play, with the exception of Mary and Joseph and the innkeepers. Try this once more and then go straight into the play.

Remind everyone that they sit down after the narrator says, *I think we all need a rest!* (Mary and Joseph remain standing, of course, and the innkeepers stand to answer the door.)

Remind the angels to jump up quickly when the narrator says, *It's Jesus' birthday today and the angels are very excited!*

Ask the innkeepers to be ready to join the party in the stable at the end of the play.

If the mechanics of the play are all in place, concentrate more on the acting.

At the end of the rehearsal, give the children lots of praise and tell them you think that everyone in the audience will love their play.

## closing prayer

*Father God, thank you for the angels*
*who were so excited about baby Jesus*
*and the shepherds who hurried to see him in the*
*manger.*
*This week, help us to be so happy and excited*
*that lots of people will hurry to see baby Jesus in*
*our play.*
***Amen***

## Memos for the play day

- Read 'It's the play day!'
- Take the *Simon Says* list from page 32 and use it to 'warm up' your actors
- Take any 'thank you' presents or cards for your helpers
- Take some spare dressing-up clothes in case anyone forgets to come in costume

# * It's the play day! *

The children will be very excited when they arrive in their costumes. Today is the climax of five weeks' hard work, so make sure that you and your helpers convey just how special today is and how much fun it will be performing the play.

You may have enough time for one last rehearsal before the performance. If not, it is essential to 'warm up' the children. Play *Simon Says* again and sing some of the carols. Get them to chant *Come to a party* from the beginning of the play several times, so that it gets off to a confident start.

Some of the children will be feeling nervous, so try to reassure them. Explain that you will be standing at the front as usual, doing all the actions. All they need to do is watch you.

Tell them that the mums and dads want to see lots of smiling faces.

During the play, don't be afraid to give any prompts quickly and loudly if the children are hesitant in front of an audience. No one should expect a perfect performance from such young children.

Check that the stage is properly set up and that you have hidden the baby doll and the star as usual.

If the shepherds and kings are carrying lambs and gifts, make sure that they put them on the floor before you start the play. Otherwise they won't have their hands free to do the actions.

## It's time, everybody!

- Make sure that the children have all been to the toilet.
- Line everyone up in the right order.

When everyone is quiet, you may like to say this prayer:

## A prayer for our play

*Father God, please bless our nativity play.*
*Give us smiling faces and big loud voices*
*    so that everyone will be able to hear the story of*
*    the first Christmas.*
*Please help us to remind everyone*
*    that Christmas is Jesus' birthday.*
***Amen***

On you go! Smile... and **enjoy yourselves!**

# Come to a PARTY!

## by Vicki Howie

**All file on to stage in this order: Mary and Joseph, kings, angels, shepherds, and innkeepers. Mary and Joseph sit on the two chairs. The innkeepers sit on the cushions. Everyone else remains standing.**

**Narr:** Birthdays are wonderful!
We ask our friends to a party…

**All:** Come to a party…
*(All beckon to audience)*

**Narr:** We blow up balloons…
*(All blow three times)*
We eat ice-cream and jelly…
*(All mime eating and say 'Mmm')*
And, if we've got any puff left, we blow out all the candles on a cake.
One, two, three, BLOW! …
*(All blow once)*
Well done!
Christmas is one big party for Jesus because it's **his** birthday…
Let's sing 'Someone's coming'.

**CAROL: Someone's coming**
**(to the tune of Frère Jacques)**

*Someone's coming*
*Someone's coming*
*A baby boy (rock baby in arms)*
*A baby boy!*
*Listen to our story (cup right ear)*
*Listen to our story (cup left ear)*
*Of great joy (hands on heart)*
*Of great joy!*

**Narr:** This is the story of the very first Christmas party… It all began when God sent the angel Gabriel to tell Mary some exciting news…
*(Angel Gabriel comes forward)*

**Gab:** Hello, Mary! Don't be afraid! God wants you to have a special baby called Jesus!
*(Angel Gabriel returns to his/her place)*

**Narr:** Mary was very happy…
*(Mary stands, smiles and clasps hands)*
But just when the baby was ready to be born, Mary and Joseph had to go on a long journey to Bethlehem.

**CAROL: Here we go up to Bethlehem**

**During the singing, Mary and Joseph walk across the stage, round behind the children, and back to where they started.**

**Narr:** What a long walk! I think we all need a rest!
*(All sit except Mary and Joseph. Innkeepers stand up)*
Bethlehem was buzzing with people…
*(All buzz and flap elbows)*
It was bursting at the seams! Where would Mary and Joseph stay for the night? They knock on a door…

**All:** Rat-a-tat-tat, rat-a-tat-tat!
*(All knock in air)*

**Narr:** But the grumpy innkeeper says…

**Inn1:** No, I haven't any room. Go away!

**Narr:** They knock on another door…

**All:** Rat-a-tat-tat, rat-a-tat-tat!
*(All knock in air)*

**Narr:** But another grumpy innkeeper says…

**Inn2:** Can't you read my sign? No room!

**Narr:** Desperately they knock on one last door…

**All:** Rat-a-tat-tat, rat-a-tat-tat!
*(All knock in air)*

**Narr:** And the very kind innkeeper says…

**Inn3:** Would you like to stay in my stable? I hope you like animals!

**He shows them the stable and they sit down—the innkeepers sit back down on their cushions.**

**CAROL: Rat-a-tat-tat, rat-a-tat-tat!**

**Narr:** That night, stars glowed like birthday candles in the night sky…
*(All raise hands and wriggle fingers)*

21

And that night, God sent us the best present we've ever had. He sent us his Son, the baby Jesus.
*(An angel walks round to give Mary a baby doll, and then returns to her place)*
There was no cot for the baby, so Mary laid him gently in the manger...
*(Mary cuddles the doll and then puts it in the manger)*

**CAROL: Away in a manger**

**Narr:** It's Jesus' birthday today and the angels are very excited! ...
*(The angels spring up, then jump up and down and clap in excitement)*
They play 'Follow my leader' all the way to the stable roof...
*(Angel Gabriel leads the angels to stand behind Mary and Joseph)*
And they hang up a big shiny star as if to say...

**All:** The party is here! ...
*(Angels hold up the big star)*

**Narr:** But who can they invite? Everyone's asleep! ...
*(All rest heads on hands)*
Everyone **except** some shepherds on the hillside. Two glowing angels fly down with a party invitation...
*(Two angels glide forward to stand in front of the shepherds)*

**Ang 1:** Dear shepherds, Please come to a party for baby Jesus!

**Ang 2:** You'll find him lying in a manger. Love, the angels.

**Narr:** The shepherds reply...

**Shep:** Yes, please! We'd love to come!

**Narr:** And they hurry after the angels with a lamb under their arms as a birthday present for the baby...

**The two angels return to their places and the chief shepherd leads the others to look in the manger and then kneel beside it.**

**CAROL: A starry night**

**Narr:** Far away in the East, some kings see the birthday star...
*(Kings point to the star)*
...and follow its twinkling lights all the way to the manger, with presents of gold, frankincense and myrrh...
*(They walk over to the manger and kneel beside it)*

**CAROL: Lift up lightly the stable bar *or* We three kings**

**Narr:** What a wonderful time they all had, talking and laughing, and opening presents... but most of all, admiring the baby Jesus!
But you don't have to be a king to come to the birthday party. Everyone is invited, rich and poor, young and old. Come on, innkeepers! ...
*(Innkeepers join the nativity scene)*
So this year, when you blow up your Christmas balloons...
*(All blow three times)*
...and eat your Christmas cake...
*(All mime eating and say 'Mmm')*
...and blow out your Christmas candles...
*(All blow once)*
...don't forget to sing Happy Birthday to Jesus.
After all, it is his birthday!

**CAROL: Happy Birthday to you!**

# THE END

## christmas crackers activity sheet

# Birthday survey!

January
February
March
April
May
June
July
August
September
October
November
December 25

What is your name?
My name is _____.
How old are you?
I am _____ years old.
What date is your birthday?
My birthday is on

_____.

Have you ever had a
birthday party? _____.
We celebrate Jesus' birthday
on _____.

Can you answer some questions?

# What's alike?

Look at my photos!

My birthday party!

My Christmas party!

Christmas
is really a big party to
celebrate Jesus' birthday. In the photos
there are five things which help Sam to celebrate both
his birthday *and* Christmas. Can you find them? Now colour them in!

# Snip! Snip!

Lucy has been cutting up some old Christmas and birthday cards to make tags for Christmas presents and birthday presents.

Can you decide which ones belong in which box? Draw arrows to help Lucy.

---

# Happy Birthday to you!

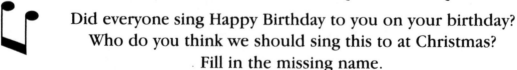

Did everyone sing Happy Birthday to you on your birthday?
Who do you think we should sing this to at Christmas?
Fill in the missing name.

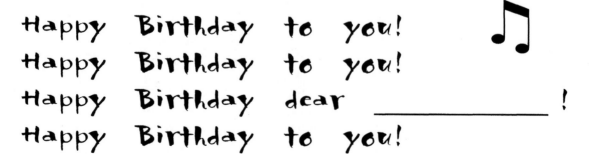

Happy Birthday to you!
Happy Birthday to you!
Happy Birthday dear _____ !
Happy Birthday to you!

## A birthday card for Jesus

... we say

# Happy Birthday, Jesus!

with lots of love, from

Stick to inside of card

Stick to front at X, Y and Z

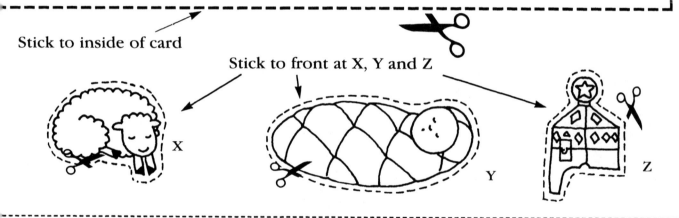

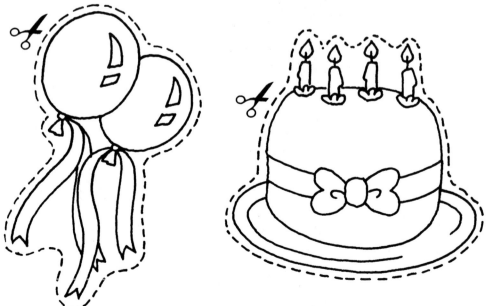

Optional extras for inside of

**Snowflakes and Robins activity sheet**

AT CHRISTMAS.

X

Y

Z

The angels have a message for Mary...

christmas crackers activity sheet

Hello, Mary!
Don't be _____

_____

_____

_____

_____

What do you think the angel is saying to Mary? Fill in the bubble. Here are some words to help you.

God loves you

afraid

a special baby

Son of God

name will be

call him Jesus

...and an invitation for the shepherds!

Can you help the angel to finish this party invitation to the shepherds?

COME TO A PARTY!

Dear shepherds,
Please _____

Time: _____

Place: _____

From _____

stable

now!

baby Jesus

today!  Bethlehem

lot of fun!

hurry!

Here are some words to help you!

27

# The innkeepers say, 'No room!'

FULL

No,

## A grumpy innkeeper!

When Mary and Joseph arrive in Bethlehem, it is very crowded. They knock on lots of doors, looking for a room for the night. But everywhere is full. What do you think this grumpy innkeeper is saying to Mary and Joseph? Fill in the bubble.

NO ROOM

Not again!

## Another grumpy innkeeper!

This innkeeper has no room either. What do you think *he* is saying? Fill in the bubble.

## A very kind innkeeper!

At last one innkeeper has a very good idea! What do you think it is? Fill in the bubble.

SORRY, NO ROOM

## Some helpful words

read my sign     my rooms are full

I have no room

hope you like animals

can't stay here     warm and dry

stay in my stable     go away

so tired     thank you

**Can you read the angel's message?**

**Snowflakes activity sheet**

Dear  _ _ _ _ _ _ _ _ ,
You are invited to a birthday party for _ _ _ _ _ _ _ _ _ _ in the _ _ _ _ _ of Bethlehem. You will find him wrapped in _ _ _ _ _ _ _ and lying in a _ _ _ _ _ _ .
Please hurry to the party! With love from the _ _ _ _ _ _ .

Manger

Baby Jesus

Town

Shepherds

**What did the shepherds reply?**

Dear _ _ _ _ _ _ ,
We would ♡ to Come to the Party for _ _ _ _ _ . We will hurry down the _ _ _ _ into the _ _ _ _ to find him lying in a _ _ _ _ _ _ . Love from the _ _ _ _

Love

Angel

Hill

Cloths

29

# Where is the party?

Colour in the clue to help Ben and his mummy.

## Where is baby Jesus?

Can you draw a line to help the kings find the birthday party?

Find God's clue and colour it in.

## I would like to be...

Draw yourself in the picture frame.

ME

An angel

A king

A shepherd

## Paper-cup characters

**King**

**Angel**

Robins activity sheet

**Shepherd**

**Wings**

Stick to upside-down cup

Stick to upside-down cup

**Camel**

Stick to upside-down cup

Baa! Baa!

**Lamb**

## Activity sheet: Forfeits for Pass the Parcel

### For everyone

Sing the first verse of 'Away in a manger' very quietly and beautifully!

### For Mary

Go and give baby Jesus a cuddle and then tuck him up again in the manger—very gently, remember!

### For Joseph

Take Mary on a long journey around the pass-the-parcel circle. Remember to look tired.

### For everyone

Rat-a-tat-tat!

Pretend to knock on a door and say,

Rat-a-tat-tat,
Rat-a-tat-tat!

One, two, three…

### For the glowing angels

Fly around until you find a shepherd. Ask him to a party for baby Jesus. Don't forget to say where it is.

### For the angel Gabriel

Go and tell Mary the exciting news about baby Jesus. Did you smile and speak in a loud voice?

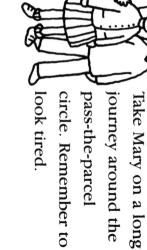
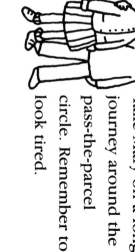
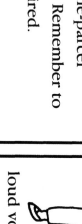

# Simon says

Blow up balloons
**(all blow three times)**

Eat ice-cream and jelly
**(all mime eating and say 'Mm')**

Blow out all the candles on a cake. One, two three, BLOW!
**(all blow once)**

Do some buzzing
**(all buzz and flap elbows)**

Make glowing stars
**(all raise hands and wriggle fingers)**

Sit down quietly

Stand up quietly

Go to sleep
**(all rest heads on hands)**

Point to a star
**(all point to the sky)**

## Activity sheet: Costumes

**Colour in Daniel and Sarah and their dressing-up clothes!**

Paste on to thin card. Cut them out and dress them up.

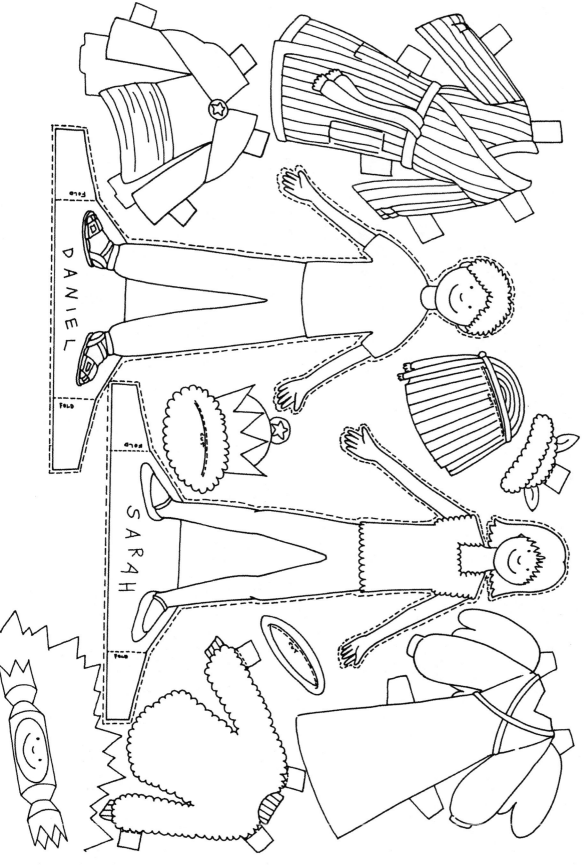

I am _____ in our nativity play! Please help me to find some dressing-up clothes.

## Poster

------------------------------------------------

# Come to a PARTY!

**Performed by:** _____

**on:** _____ **at:** _____

**place:** _____

**Please bring:** _____

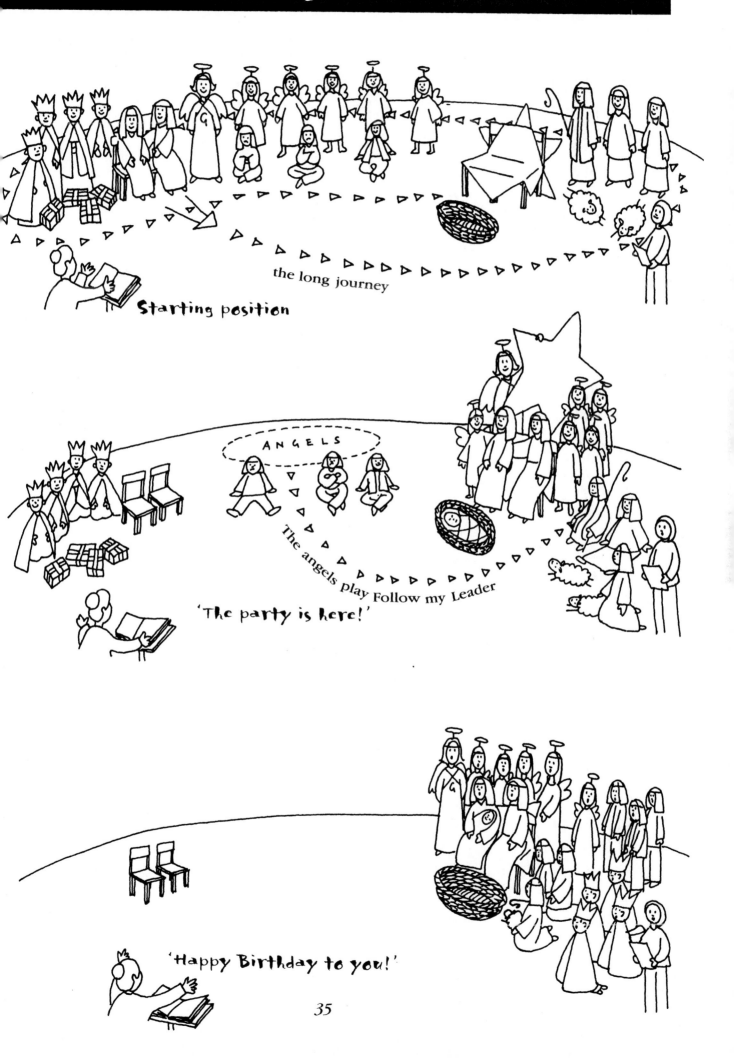

the long journey

**Starting position**

ANGELS

The angels play Follow my Leader

'The party is here!'

'Happy Birthday to you!'

# THE STAR
## who couldn't
# TWINKLE

# INTRODUCTION

This nativity play is all about a little star who cannot sparkle or shine because he is too shy to look up at God's beaming smile. He asks the other stars and a glowing angel for help, but no one can stop his light fading—until Jesus is born, wearing God's saving smile on his face! In this very simple way, it introduces the idea that Jesus was born to bring us close to God.

Don't worry if you are performing this play with a number of very young children. You don't need a star-studded cast! In fact, one of the advantages of this play is that the star, who can be played by an adult helper or an older child, leads the other characters to wherever they need to go on the stage. All the younger ones need do is to *follow that star*!

Before you start working with the children, read through all the material and familiarize yourself with the play. Give copies of the play to your helpers so that they will know how to help the children at the very first rehearsal.

## Adapting the play to suit your group

This simple play was written specifically for a group of 3–7 year olds with only a short time to rehearse each week. It was designed to give the older ones a chance to say a line, while keeping the younger ones interested and involved throughout in actions and mimes.

Apart from giving the part of the star to an adult, you can further simplify the play by leaving out the 'smiley faces' which the older shepherds and kings hold up at various points. You could also integrate any or all of the speaking parts into the narration and simply let the children mime the story.

Conversely, you could add more speaking parts with an older group, by giving lines to the shepherds and kings and having a group of animals in the stable who complain that they want their dinner. The narration can also be divided between several children.

## Casting

At this stage, it is helpful to have some idea about who will play the main parts, so you may like to pencil in some possible names beside the list of main characters below. (The activities in the 'Four weeks to go' section of the countdown, on pages 44–45, will help you to make a final choice and to divide the rest of the children into three groups of shepherds, kings and stars.)

### Main characters

*The narrator*—a leader or helper if your group consists of young children
*The little star*—a leader or helper, or confident older child
*The glowing angel*—a confident older child
*Mary and Joseph, Sparkle and Glow (two stars), and the innkeeper*—five children who would enjoy speaking parts

The remaining children are shepherds, kings or stars.

## Essential props

Benches for the shepherds and kings
Two chairs
A box or basket for the manger
A baby doll (with a smiling face, if possible) to represent Jesus
A small blanket
A small star on a stick with a sad face—use the template on page 54 and the ideas on page 60 to make your own.

A big shiny star cut from very thick card and covered in foil. You can copy the shape on the activity sheet, page 54. Add a smiling face—and hands and feet if you wish.

## After the performance

If you are having refreshments after the performance, you may like to carry on with the 'star' theme by having a Galaxy Café appropriately decorated and using star-studded paper tablecloths, etc.

## Memos for next week

• Read 'Five weeks to go'
• Take along some sparklers and matches *or* a star, shiny on one side and black on the other

- Photocopy the activity sheets you want to use and cut out the items for the 'Can you make me twinkle?' picture, ready for the younger children

Depending on your choice of activities, you may need:

- an old microphone (or improvise with a cardboard roll)
- glitter
- two piles of instructions and excuses for 'Excruciating excuses'
- paper (perhaps cut into star shapes) on which the children can 'Pen a prayer'

## Five weeks to go – Introducing the theme of the play

This week, the aim is to read the story *The star who couldn't twinkle* to the children and to emphasize that Jesus came to bring us close to God.

With everyone sitting at a safe distance, light a sparkler and make patterns by waving it in a circle or figure of eight. Encourage everyone to 'ooh!' and 'aah!' Make sure the children are watching carefully as it fades, splutters and finally goes out.

Point out how exciting it was when the sparkler was burning brightly and how sad it was when it started to go out.

Alternatively, use the star shape on page 54 to make a star from thin card. Decorate one side with glitter or foil and colour the reverse black. Ask the children which looks the most like a twinkling star. Hold the shiny side to the light and point out how it sparkles; then turn it over and say that the light has gone out.

Ask everyone to stand up. Say, *Can you sparkle like the firework/shiny side of the star? Hold out your arms ... wiggle your fingers ... turn round in a circle. Brilliant! What lovely twinkling lights! Now start to fade ... stop wiggling those fingers ... crouch down ... now fade a bit more. Kneel down, everyone ... and, oh dear, we're going out ... sit down ... we've gone out!*

Explain that you're going to tell them a story about a little star who was very sad because he couldn't sparkle or twinkle.

Read *The star who couldn't twinkle*, making sure that everyone can see the pictures.

## The star who couldn't twinkle

There was once a little star who couldn't twinkle.
He was sad about that.
Stars are supposed to twinkle.
'Can you tell me how to twinkle?' he asked his sparkling brothers and sisters.
'You must find God, who made you,' they said. 'Look at his golden smile. Then you will start to twinkle.'
But the little star was too shy.
'Excuse me. Can *you* make me twinkle?' he asked a glowing angel.

'I'm sorry. Only God can do that, with his beaming smile,' said the angel. 'Have a look for him. He's never far away.'
'I'm a bit too busy today,' said the little star.
'And I must fly,' said the angel. 'I've got a message for Mary.'
The little star slid down the heavens to find Mary.
'Hello, Mary!' said the little star. 'You look happy and bright. Can you help me to twinkle?'
'No!' said Mary. 'But I can tell you some wonderful news. I'm going to have a baby. He will be the Son of God and we must call him Jesus!'
'Can I stay and see the baby?' asked the little star.
'Certainly!' said Mary. 'You'll have to wait a bit. But you can help Joseph with the cot.'

'It's bad news,' said Joseph one day. 'We must go all the way to Bethlehem to pay our taxes.'
'Can I come with you?' asked the little star. 'I don't want to miss the baby.'
The little star travelled ahead of them on the long journey.
Mary's back ached.
Joseph's feet ached.
And the little star ached all over with trying to light the bumpy road.
At last he saw Bethlehem in the distance.
'The streets are full of people,' he called down.
Joseph looked worried.
'I hope we can find a room for the night,' he said.

40

The little star watched his friends knock on one door after another. But the answer was always, 'No room, no room!'
'Hurry up with our dinner,' said the cows in a shed by an inn.
The innkeeper was filling their manger with hay.
'Excuse me,' said the little star. 'Can my friends stay the night in your shed?'
'Yes, all right!' said the innkeeper.
'They do look tired.'
The little star made sure that Mary and Joseph were safe and warm.
Then he gave a great yawn and fell asleep.
In the night, a strange sound woke him.
It was coming from the manger.
It was a baby crying!
The little star hung as low as he dared over the manger.
The baby stopped crying and smiled at him.
What a smile!
It washed over him like a golden wave.
He was swimming in light!
He was sparkling with gold dust!
He was growing … he was glowing …

**HE WAS TWINKLING!**

'Ah, that's better!' said the angel.

'I'm just going to tell those shepherds where to find the baby Jesus. Could you point a finger of light?'

'What a star!' said the wise men.

'It must belong to a great new king. Let's follow it!'

That night, the twinkling Christmas star shone with happiness.

'Who made you twinkle like that?' asked Mary, smiling.

'God did!' said the Christmas star. 'He sent his smile into the world on the face of the baby Jesus. Wasn't that kind!'

# Activity time

Divide the children into groups according to which activity you want them to do.

## The Christmas crackers

### Star excuses

When the children have found the appropriate excuses, you could interview them about *their* favourite excuses, using your microphone! Say, *Is there anything you don't like doing, Richard? What do you say to get out of it?*

Who's got the funniest excuse?

### Who made him twinkle?

You may like to discuss the answers to the clues and look at the story again with the children, before asking them to fill in the answers on the crossword.

Point out that God is very sad when people turn away from him like the little star did at the beginning of the story, but that God loves us so much, he sent Jesus into the world to help us make friends again with God.

## Snowflakes and robins

### Can *you* make me twinkle?

Both groups can do this activity, but be sure to do the cutting out for the younger ones. If you have time, the children can colour the pictures before sticking them down.

Hold up the main picture and remind the children that the star is very sad because he can't twinkle. Give out the sparkling stars and say, *Let's see if his brothers and sisters can make him twinkle. Stick them in the sky … that's it … No! He's still not twinkling!*

Do the same with the glowing angel and say, *No! The angel says that only God can make the little star twinkle.*

Repeat with Mary, and then, when you stick the manger on to the picture, say, *Here's baby Jesus! He's brought God's smile into the world. Now the little star will twinkle. Let's give him a happy face!*

The children can colour him brightly and add glitter, if you are feeling brave!

## Further ideas

### Excruciating excuses

Write down the instructions below on separate pieces of paper and put them in a pile. Make another pile of the corresponding excuses. Tell the children that you want one of your helpers to do some small jobs for you, but that he or she keeps making excuses. Ask them to listen as you read out all the instructions, with your helper giving the corresponding excuse each time. Now shuffle the two piles and make the children laugh as you read them all out again, this time in the wrong order! If you have some good readers in the group, let pairs of children take turns at this. Shuffle the two piles again each time.

**Instructions / *Excuses***

Put that spider out of the back door.
*I can't! He's got eight hairy legs!*

Take the dog for a walk.
*I can't! I've lost his lead.*

Go and help Grandad dig the garden.
*I can't! He's mowing the lawn.*

Please feed the cat.
*Not now! He's chasing a mouse.*

Help your little brother with his homework.
*Not now! He's playing on his toy trumpet.*

Clean out the budgie's cage.
*No! I'm afraid he might peck me.*

Put the goldfish in clean water.
*No! He's too slippery.*

Hold the hamster for me.
*No! He might have fleas.*

### Pen a prayer

Ask the older ones to write a prayer asking God to help them with anything they find difficult to do. Explain that God loves us and wants to help us to shine. He may even have a very important job for us to do, as he did for the little star.

You could ask the younger ones about anything they can't do, and then say a prayer incorporating their ideas; for example:
*Dear God,*
*Please help Laura to hop; please help David to write his name …*
*Amen*

Include something that *you* find difficult!

## Closing prayer

*Dear God,*
*Thank you for loving us.*
*Thank you for sending baby Jesus into the world*
*    with your loving smile.*
*Help us to shine brightly for you*
*    just like the Christmas star!*
**Amen**

## Memos for next week

- Read 'Four weeks to go'
- Read the play again and study the 'starting position' for all the children
- Make sure you have the essential props ready to use straight away. (Try to set up the stage before the children arrive.)
- If possible, take a music stand to put the play on when you are directing the action
- Copy the paper plate faces to illustrate your retelling of the little star story. You will also need your little star on a stick and the big shiny star from the essential props
- Photocopy the activity sheets
- Cut out card circles for the badges and tape safety-pins to one side. Cut out enough star, shepherd and king badges for the children to choose from

Using the little star on a stick and the big shiny star, retell the little star story in your own words, emphasizing the feelings of the characters. As you do this, ask six children to hold up some paper plate faces with simple expressions as shown to illustrate the story. Ask, *Why was Mary happy and bright? ... What kind thing did the innkeeper do? etc.*

# 5 4 3 2 1

# Four weeks to go— Introducing the characters

The aim this week is to get the children thinking about the different characters in the story; what they did and how they felt. The activities will help everyone to decide who they want to be in the play before you start the first rehearsal.

# Activity time

## The Christmas crackers

### Play your part!

Give this sheet to those children you think will be playing the main parts. Have fun letting everyone read the various parts in the six situations, then make a final decision about who everyone is going to be, and make a note of this. Try to take into account the children's own wishes. Make sure they all take a sheet home to start learning their words.

# Snowflakes and Robins

### Biblical badges

Each child can make a badge to show whether they'd like to be a star, shepherd or king in the play. Ask everyone to colour the picture

before sticking it on to the card. While they colour, remind them of the parts played by each group in the story. Pin on their badges ready for the play rehearsal.

## It's play time!

Put the benches, chairs, and manger in position if you haven't already done so. (See stage plan on page 63.) The two chairs should be slightly apart to leave room for the star on a stick to be dangled over the manger. Hide the big star behind one of the two chairs, and the baby doll under a small blanket in the manger.

Take each group of shepherds and kings to go and sit on the appropriate bench and ask the innkeeper to sit on a chair. Mary and Joseph and the glowing angel should stand on opposite sides of the stage as shown. The stars stand in a group behind the kings (together with the little star) ready to come forward at the appropriate moment. (Grit your teeth! Getting everyone in the right starting position takes time!)

If possible, have an adult helper with each group. Appoint a chief star, shepherd and king to be responsible for helping the younger ones.

Ask everyone to watch you and to copy what you do. Then, as the narrator starts to read the play, lead the children in the mimes. Smile, give lots of encouragement, and act as you would if you were getting everyone to play an enjoyable party game!

(Leave the smiley faces until next week.)

As yet, the children will be hesitant when given any instruction to move around the stage, so step forward, take a hand and walk with them. (The activities for next week will help to build their confidence.)

Make sure that your narrator pauses long enough to allow for the mimes or other actions, but also keeps the story going fairly briskly. The children will lose interest if there are long gaps.

Sing any carols the children already know at the appropriate moments. Otherwise, say, *This is where we'll sing... which we're going to learn later on.*

If you don't have time for the whole play (and you probably won't!), remind the children of the way the story ends and get each group to practise following the star to the manger. Make a note to start where you left off next week.

## Closing prayer

*Lord Jesus,*
*Thank you for watching over us all the time,*
*    whether we are happy like Mary,*
*    or worried like Joseph,*
*    or sad, like the little star in the story.*
*Help us to be like the shepherds and the kings,*
*    always walking towards you!*
**Amen**

## Memos for next week

- Read 'Three weeks to go'
- Make and take a Christmas star from the activity sheet. (Use the template on page 54.)
- Photocopy the activity sheet and take craft materials if the children are to make their own Christmas stars
- Draw some smiling faces on paper plates, enough for the older shepherds and kings and one for yourself. Take some plain ones if the children are to draw their own

## Three weeks to go – Reach for the stars!

The aim this week is to encourage the children to think how they can shine in life by keeping healthy physically, mentally and spiritually. At the same time, they'll be practising some of the actions in the play.

Say, *Put up your hand if you'd like to be a star ... What kind of star would you like to be? Would anyone like to be a star at football? ... Who'd like to be a television star? ... Would anyone like to be a star swimmer? Well, I've brought someone with me who can tell you how to be a real star. Here he is—it's the Christmas star.*

Bring out your shiny star, complete with face, hands and feet and the words 'body', 'brain', and 'belief' written on stickers and taped on to him. Pretend to interview the star, telling him that all the children want to know how to shine, and asking him for advice. Explain to the children that the star says they need to do three things. Number one is to keep their *bodies* fit. Ask everyone to stand up to do some star-obics!

### Star-obics

Ask the children to spread out like stars in the sky. Make sure they don't touch anyone else when they stretch their arms out to the sides.

Now get them to do a short keep-fit routine, starting with very gentle movements to warm up. (Do each of the following about five times.)

- Look at your feet, then look up at the stars…
- Roll your shoulders up near your ears, then back…
- Bend over to touch your toes, then slowly uncurl…
- Jog on the spot…
- Feet apart … now reach for the stars … and jump your feet together and apart again … that's it, star jumps!
- Now let's cool down by walking … find a partner and hold hands … everyone ready? … Then off we go … let's walk quickly at first … now start to slow down … now we're feeling very tired … we're hardly moving … oooh, my back hurts, rub your backs … and my legs ache, give your legs a rub … in fact, rub everything … yawn, and sit down for a rest.

### What a smile!

Now that they've exercised their bodies, the Christmas star says that everyone must exercise their *brains* if they want to be stars. Ask two of the older shepherds and kings to come out to the front and give each of them a paper plate with a smiley face on it. Explain that you are going to read them a poem about the play. Every time they hear the word 'smile' or 'smiled', they must hold up their smiley faces. Ask the others to listen carefully and make sure no one has an upside-down smile!

Read 'What a smile!' from the activity sheet (page 60). Try the poem again, this time with different children holding up the smiley faces. You could get the others to draw imaginary smiles on their faces for the word 'smile(d)', and wiggle their fingers like twinkling stars for the word 'twinkle'. Get them to cover their faces with their hands for 'he hid his face from sight'. You could turn the poem into a 'rap' and perform it at the end of the play as an encore.

### Follow the star

Now that you've exercised your bodies and your brains, ask the Christmas star what the third thing is that you need to do to be a star in life. He says that the answer is to keep your face turned towards God (keeping your *belief* in God strong) and that this is the most important thing of all. Remind everyone that the little star almost faded away because he wouldn't look up at God. Explain that you can do this by talking to God (or praying) every day, by reading Bible stories, by coming to Sunday school or church, etc.

Finish the session by playing 'Follow the star'. Ask the adult or child who is going to play the little star to walk round the room with the Christmas star held up high. Gradually get everyone to fall in behind him or her in this order: the glowing angel, the shepherds, the innkeeper, the kings, Mary and Joseph, and the stars (including Sparkle and Glow). You are now in the right order to lead on to the stage for a rehearsal. Get the star to drop everyone off in the right place (see stage plan, page 63).

## Further ideas

The children could make their own Christmas star to remind them about all they've learned or they could make their own paper plate smiley faces.

## It's play time!

If you stopped halfway through the play last week and you are running short of time, quickly talk and walk the children up to that point before starting in earnest.

This week, the older shepherds and kings can hold up their smiley faces at the appropriate moments. You could hold one up yourself to remind them. Call out 'Follow the star' when the two groups go to the manger, and get them to leave the paper plates on the benches. (The glowing angel will need to pick up one of these to hold up at the end of the play.)

Be encouraging and don't worry if it seems to you as if the play will never be ready. It will, so concentrate on making the rehearsal good fun!

## Closing prayer

*Father God, we want to be your sparkling stars.*
*Help us to keep our bodies fit and healthy,*
*    our brains busy,*
*    and our faces always turned towards you.*
**Amen**

## Memos for next week

- Read 'Two weeks to go'
- Take any pictures you can find of biblical costumes

- Photocopy the activity sheet from page 61
- Decide which of the 'Further ideas' you want to tackle and take the appropriate materials

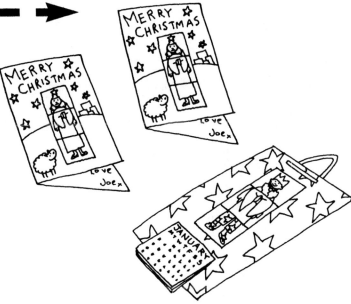

## Two weeks to go - costumes and props

This week, try to leave more time for practising the play.

Give parents advance warning (perhaps via the activity sheets) that you'd like the children to come dressed in an appropriate *simple* costume on the day of the play.

Look at pictures of the biblical characters in the nativity story with the children, either in books or on Christmas cards, and ask them to suggest what they could find at home to dress up in (see page 18).

Ask the stars whether they have anything sparkly to wear, such as tights or hair slides. Suggest white T-shirts or blouses over white tights, with tinsel round their heads and waists. Or they may like to make the star headbands described under the 'Further ideas' section.

## Activity time

The activity sheets will help to remind the children to look for dressing-up clothes at home.

## Further ideas

The children could make **star headbands** by attaching a star, covered in foil or cut from yellow card, to a card headband.

Play the **dressing-up game** described on page 18.

Use the heads, shoulders, knees and toes pictures on the activity sheet on page 61 to make a **collage or individual Christmas cards, calendars or bookmarks**.

## It's play time!

Try to go through the entire play this week so that the children have a complete run through. Sing all the carols at the appropriate moments.

At the end, practise all the chants marked 'All' such as 'Rumble, rumble!' and 'No room, no room!' giving the children their lead-in sentence first.

Be as encouraging as possible and remind yourself that it is more important for the children to have fun learning about the Christmas story than to produce a perfect play.

## Closing prayer

*Thank you, God, for all the fun we had today thinking about our dressing-up clothes.*
*Thank you for sending us your only son, Jesus, wearing your loving smile on his face.*
**Amen**

## Memos for next week

- Read 'One week to go'
- Photocopy the poster and complete the 'Please bring…' section for the youngest children
- Make sure that all your arrangements are in place for the play day, including any plans you have for refreshments afterwards
- Take card, glitter, foil, etc. for the trail of sparkling stars
- Take gummed star stickers to decorate paper cups.

## One week to go – Come to our play!

This week, be determined to leave as much time as you need to rehearse the play without letting other activities overrun.

Talk to the children about what will happen on the play day and encourage them to bring along their family and friends to watch. Make sure that everyone has found something to wear in the play. Find out if anyone can bring a toy lamb or sheep for the younger shepherds —the older ones will have the smiley faces to hold.

## Activity time

Ask all the children to colour in the poster advertising the play. The older children can fill in the missing details. Use the 'Please bring…' section as appropriate, for example, *cakes or star-shaped cookies, friends and relatives*, or simply *Sam dressed in his costume*!

### Further ideas

**Make a trail of sparkling stars** so that the audience can 'follow the star' to your hall or stage.

**Decorate some paper cups** with star stickers ready for refreshments after the performance.

### It's play time!

Play 'Follow the star' again (see page 46) with the star carrying his own little star on a stick, and practise leading quietly on to the stage area.

Before you start the play, mention a few things that everyone must be ready to do. Remind everyone to stand up when they say, *Oh no! Off we go!* and to sit down again when Mary and Joseph sit down on the two chairs. After that, the star will lead them to the manger.

Practise all the chants marked 'All' again, giving the children their lead-in sentence first.

Remind Mary to uncover the baby doll when she hears the words, 'It was coming from the manger…'

Once these mechanics have all been put in place, concentrate on the acting.

At the end of the rehearsal, give the children lots of praise and tell them you think that everyone in the audience will love their play.

### Closing prayer

*Father God, thank you for helping us
    with our play today.*
*Help us to remember
    that you need each one of us
    to tell the story about baby Jesus.*
*Thank you that we are all special to you.*
***Amen***

### Memos for the play day

- Read 'It's the play day!'
- Photocopy 'What a smile' from page 60 to warm up your actors
- Take any 'thank you' presents or cards for helpers
- Take some spare dressing-up clothes in case anyone forgets to come in costume

## * It's the play day! *

The children are bound to be very excited when they arrive in their costumes. Join in with their excitement and make today a special one.

If you don't have time for one last rehearsal, it's vital to warm up by singing some songs from the play and practising the chants. You could also get the children to do the actions to 'What a smile!'

Reassure any nervous children and remind them that you will be standing at the front as usual, doing all the actions. All they need to do is watch you!

Remind everyone to smile and speak up loudly so that even the people in the back row can hear the story. During the play, don't be afraid to give any prompts quickly and loudly if the children are hesitant in front of an audience.

Check that the stage is set up properly, the big shiny star is hidden and the baby doll is covered up in the manger. It will spoil the atmosphere a little if you have to run on with the doll in the middle of the play!

Check that the older shepherds and kings have their smiley faces.

### It's time, everybody!

- Make sure that the children have all been to the toilet
- Line everyone up in the right order behind the little star

When everyone is quiet, you could say this prayer:

## A prayer for our play

*Father God, please bless our nativity play.*
*Give us smiling faces*
*and big loud voices*
*so that everyone will be able to hear*
*how Jesus helped the little star.*
**Amen**

On you go! Follow that star …
and **enjoy yourselves!**

# The star who couldn't TWINKLE

## by Vicki Howie

All the characters line up behind the little star to lead on to the stage in this order: the glowing angel, the shepherds, the innkeeper, the kings, Mary and Joseph, and the stars (including Sparkle and Glow).

The innkeeper sits on one of the two chairs (to be used later by Mary and Joseph), positioned towards the side of the stage. The glowing angel stands on the opposite side of the stage to Mary and Joseph. The stars wait behind the kings for their cue to walk on.

**Narr:** In the beginning, God made the stars…
*(Stars walk on to centre stage)*
…and scattered them in the sky…
*(Stars spread out between the two seated groups)*
Then God smiled at his beautiful stars…
*(Kings and shepherds hold up smiley faces)*
…and they all began to twinkle…
*(Stars rotate)*
They twinkled like the lights in God's eyes!
But this story is about a little star who *couldn't* twinkle…
*(Little star walks on from behind and stands in the middle of the stars)*
He was much too shy to look up at God's lovely smile, and so his light faded…
*(Stars crouch down)*
…and faded…
*(Stars kneel down)*
…and faded…
*(Stars sit down)*
…until he was just a tiny spot of light.

**All:** Oh dear!

**Narr:** The little star asked his sparkling brothers and sisters for some advice…

**Star:** Can you please tell me how to twinkle?

**Spark:** Look at God's smile.

**Glow:** Then you will start to twinkle.

**Narr:** But the little star hid his face from sight…
*(All cover faces)*
A glowing angel flew past the little star on his way down to the Earth…
*(The angel flies across the stage in front of the little star)*
The little star cried out to her…

**Star:** Excuse me, can *you* make me twinkle?

**Angel:** I'm sorry. Only God can do that, with his beaming smile. Have a look for him!

**Narr:** But the little star said he was too busy, and the angel had to fly with a message for Mary…
*(Angel flies over to Mary and whispers in her ear)*
The little star was so miserable that everyone sang him this song.

**CAROL: Try to twinkle, little star**

*Try to twinkle, little star,*
*Then we'll know just what you are.*
*Up above the world so high,*
*Like a diamond in the sky,*
*Try to twinkle, little star,*
*Then we'll know just what you are!*

**Narr:** The little star slid down the heavens to find Mary…
*(Star comes forward and Mary walks across to meet him)*
She was looking so happy and bright that the little star said…

**Star:** Hello, Mary! Can you help me to twinkle?

**Mary:** No! But I can tell you some wonderful news. God sent an angel to tell me I'm going to have a baby called Jesus!

**Narr:** The little star clapped his hands in delight, he was so happy.

50

**CAROL: If you're happy and you know it, clap your hands!**

Narr: How exciting! A new baby! But just when the baby was going to be born, Joseph had some bad news to tell Mary…
*(Joseph walks towards Mary)*

Jose: I'm sorry, but we must go all the way to Bethlehem to pay our taxes.

All: Oh, no! Off we go!
*(All stand up)*

Narr: The little star travelled ahead of them on the long journey…
*(Star leads Mary and Joseph around the stage, quickly at first and then slower and slower)*
Mary's back ached…
*(All rub backs and groan)*
…Joseph's legs ached…
*(All rub legs and groan)*
…and the little star ached all over with trying to light the bumpy road!
*(All rub everything and groan!)*

**The star leads tired Mary and Joseph around the stage while all sing…**

**CAROL: Little donkey**

Narr: At last, the little star saw Bethlehem in the distance…
*(All shade eyes and stare)*
The streets were full of people and he wondered if they would find a room for the night. Mary and Joseph knocked on one door after another…

All: Knock, knock!
*(All knock in air)*

Narr: But the answer was always…

All: No room, no room!

Narr: In a cow shed behind an inn, some donkeys and cows were getting hungry for their dinner…

All: Rumble, rumble!
*(All rub stomachs)*

Narr: The innkeeper was busy filling their manger with hay…
*(Innkeeper stands and mimes filling the manger)*
The little star peered down into the warm, dry shed…
*(The star goes to stand behind the two chairs)*
And then, very politely, he asked a question…

Star: Excuse me. Can my friends stay the night in your shed?

Narr: The innkeeper looked at Mary and Joseph… and then he nodded.

Inn: Yes, of course they can. They look so tired…

*(He gestures to the two chairs and then joins the shepherds)*

Narr: The little star made sure that Mary and Joseph were safe and warm…
*(Mary and Joseph sit down on the two chairs, and everyone else sits down)*
Then he gave a great yawn…
*(All yawn)*
…and fell asleep…
*(All rest heads on hands)*
In the night, a strange sound woke him.
It was coming from the manger…
*(Mary uncovers the baby doll)*
It was a baby crying!
The little star hung as low as he dared over the manger…
*(Star dangles the tiny star on a stick over the manger)*
The baby stopped crying and smiled at him.
What a smile!
*(All draw imaginary smiles on their own faces or hold up smiley faces)*
It washed over the little star like a golden wave.
He was swimming in light!
He was sparkling with gold dust!
He was growing … he was glowing … **he was twinkling!**

**During the last three phrases, the star puts down the tiny star on a stick and picks up the big one, which he holds above his head.**

**CAROL: This little light of mine**

Narr: The glowing angel appeared again…
*(The angel walks into the middle and turns towards the shepherds)*
…and told some shepherds out in the fields that Jesus the Saviour was born…
*(The angel walks over to the shepherds and mimes rocking a baby)*
Then the angel called to the twinkling star…

Angel: Ah, that's *much* better! Can you help these shepherds to find the baby Jesus? …
*(Angel goes to stand behind shepherd's bench)*

Narr: Gathering all his strength, the star pointed his twinkling lights towards the cow shed and watched in delight as the shepherds followed him to the smiling baby…
*(The star leads the shepherds to kneel by the manger)*

51

**CAROL: Go, tell it on the mountain**

**Narr:** Far away in the East, some kings saw a twinkling light in the sky...
*(Kings point to the star)*
'What a magnificent star!' they cried.
'It must belong to a great, new king. Let's follow it!'
The twinkling star glowed proudly when he heard the kings' words and he led them all the way to baby Jesus.

**The star leads the kings round the stage and then to kneel by the manger, while all sing...**

**CAROL: O come, little children**

**Narr:** After that, the Christmas star was never too shy to look up at God...
*(Angel holds up a smiley face)*
His light grew bigger and brighter and you can still see him twinkling in the night sky at Christmas time! How glad he is that God sent his smile into the world on the face of the baby Jesus!
*(Mary takes doll on to her lap)*

**CAROL: Shine, Jesus, shine**
     **(with audience)**


# THE END

# Star excuses

The little star said he was too shy and too busy to look for God. What excuses do you think he gives for not doing these things?

☆ Going to bed
☆ Eating his sprouts
☆ Doing his homework
☆ Cleaning his teeth
☆ Turning off the TV

What are your favourite excuses?

I'm **not hungry!**

I'm **too tired!**

I'm **not tired!**

It's my **favourite programme!**

I've **already done them!**

## ☆☆ Who made him twinkle?

Fill in the crossword and find the answer in the box.

1. The little star was _____ because he couldn't twinkle.

2. He asked a glowing _____ to make him twinkle.

3. The little star slid down the _____ to find Mary.

4. Mary couldn't make him _____ either.

5. The little star went with Mary and _____ to Bethlehem.

6. The cows in the shed said, '_____ up with our dinner!'

7. In the night, he heard _____ coming from the manger.

Now you can help the angel tell the good news!

christmas crackers
activity sheet

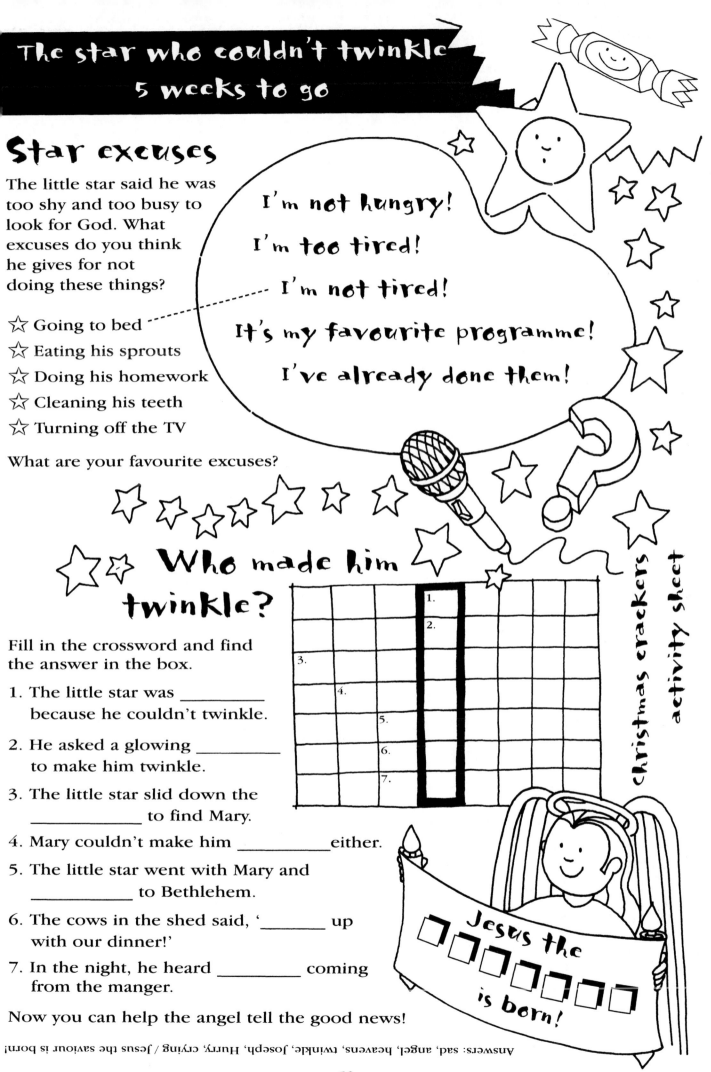

Jesus the □□□□□ is born!

## Snowflakes and Robins activity sheet
### Can YOU make me twinkle?

glowing angel

sparkling stars

Mary

smiley face

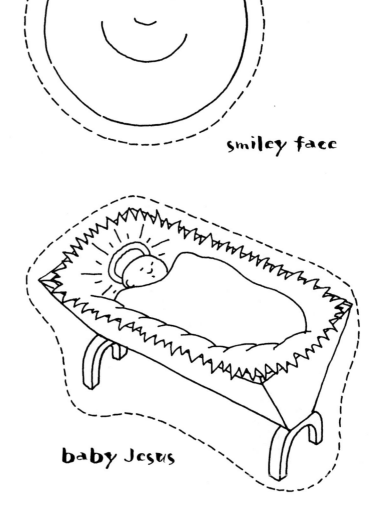

baby Jesus

## christmas crackers activity sheet
# Play your part!

56

### Snowflakes and Robins activity sheet

# Biblical badges

Colour, cut out and stick to thin card
with safety-pin attached.

Activity sheet

## What a smile!

God made the stars,
And hung them in the sky.
They all began to twinkle,
Shall I tell you why?
God smiled at his stars,
For he loved them through and through.
It's amazing what a smile can do!

> What a smile! Twinkle, twinkle!
> What a smile!  Twinkle, twinkle!
> It's amazing what a smile can do!

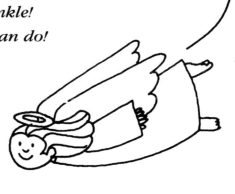

A sad little star,
Was hanging in the sky.
I'm afraid he couldn't twinkle,
Shall I tell you why?
When God smiled at his stars,
He hid his face from sight.
It's amazing how he faded to a tiny spot of light.

> What a shame! Oh dear!
> What a shame! Oh dear!
> It's amazing how that star ran out of light!

Sparkling stars couldn't help him,
Nor an angel flying by.
They couldn't make him twinkle,
Shall I tell you why?
Only baby Jesus,
With God's love upon his face,
Could brighten up the little star—and the human race!

> What a smile! Twinkle, twinkle!
> What a smile! Twinkle, twinkle!
> It's amazing how that smile lit up his face!

# Make your own Christmas star!

## Cut

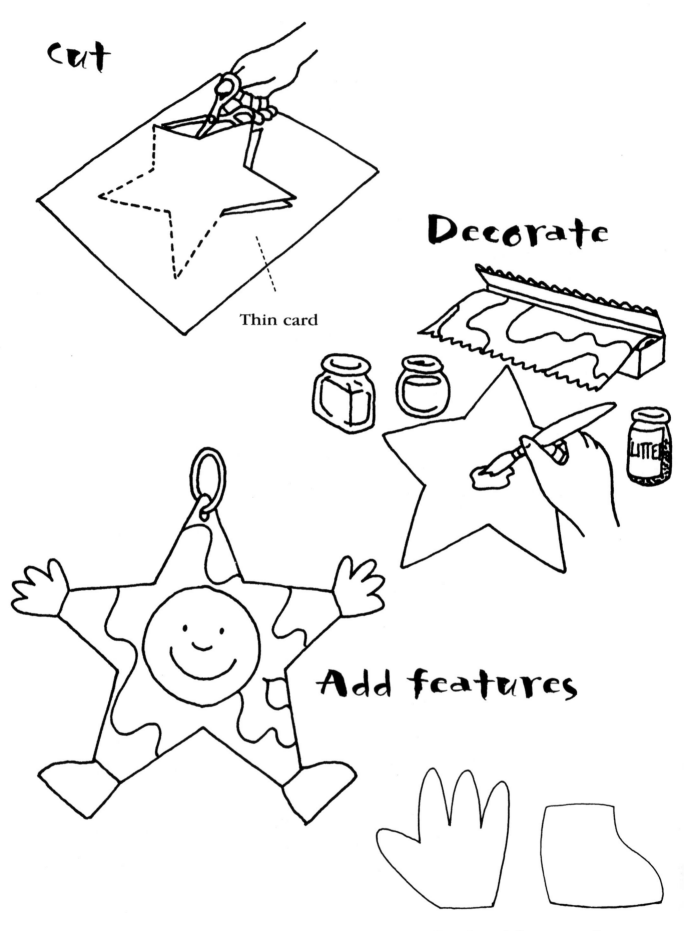

Thin card

## Decorate

## Add features

Hand and foot templates

In our play, I'm going to be . . .

Please help me find some dressing-up clothes!

# The star who couldn't twinkle – 2 weeks to go

## Activity sheet : Put yourself on the stage

Make a bookmark!

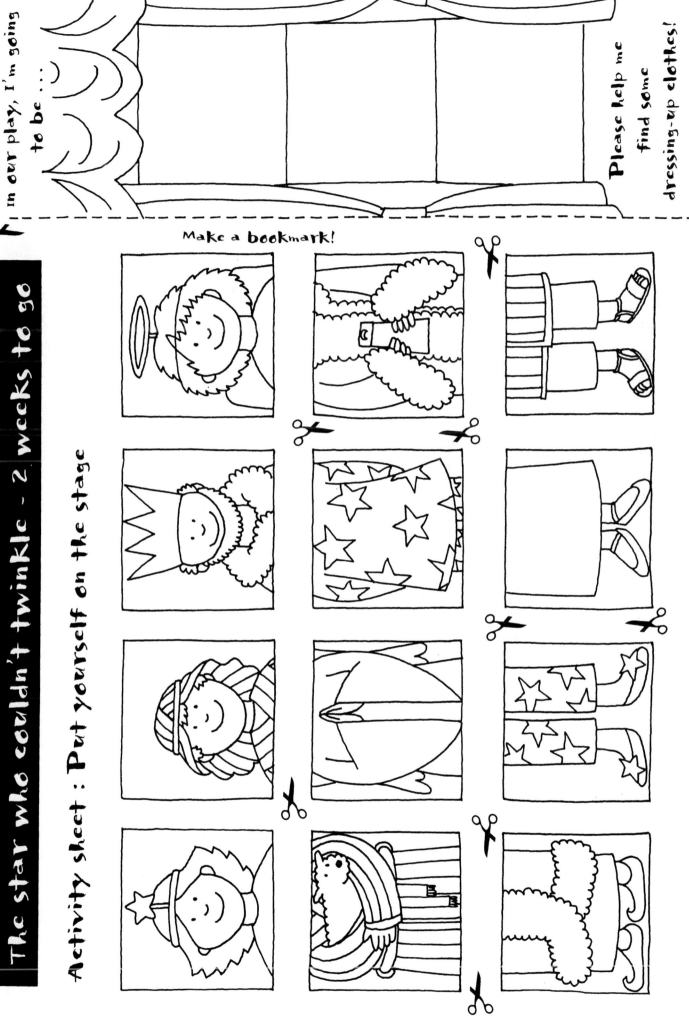

# The star who couldn't
# TWINKLE

A nativity play starring:

_____

on: _____

at:_____

place: _____

**Please bring:** _____

# Shine your LIGHTS!

# INTRODUCTION

If you are attracted by the romance of a Victorian Christmas in the country, then this is the play for you! It tells the story of some children who go carol singing on Christmas Eve while the villagers prepare busily for Chistmas Day. But as the snow starts to fall, they are amazed to see Mary and Joseph struggling into their village. The wonderful nativity story unfolds before them in the light of their lamps and brings home to them the real meaning of Christmas.

Before you start working with the children, read through all the material and familiarize yourself with the play. Give copies of the play to your helpers so that they will know how to help the children at the very first rehearsal.

## Adapting the play to suit your group

'*Shine your lights!*' is aimed at the top end of the age group and is therefore a little more challenging than the other plays in this book. It would be ideal for a class in which everyone would like a line to say or a special part to play.

It could also be performed in church, perhaps on Christmas Day, with the carol singers and a few villagers standing at the front and the nativity characters coming down the aisle and forming a tableau. The narrators (either adults or children) could read from the pulpit or a lectern. Omit the characters of the cat and the clock if you wish to simplify things.

## Casting

Look at the list of characters below and decide who will play each part. The carol singers and the four children who join them have the most to do, while the shepherds, angels and kings have the least.

### Characters

Four narrators
Four children
The cat
Several carol singers
A cook or cooks
Lord(s) and lady(ies)
Mother and children
Church clock
Victorian innkeeper
Mary and Joseph
Shepherds
Angels
Kings

## Essential props

Two chairs for the stable
Four stools for the four children
Benches or boxes for the other characters
A box or basket for the manger
A baby doll to represent Jesus
If possible, a Christmas tree, real or artificial

Suggestions are given for costumes and further props on page 77.

## After the performance

You may like to carry on the theme of the play by inviting the audience to stay on for some old-fashioned refreshments. Decorate a table with Victorian swags and bows and serve mulled wine or spicy fruit punch with warmed mince pies.

## Memos for next week

- Read 'Five weeks to go'
- Take a shopping bag with a rolling pin, a pack of Christmas cards, a Christmas angel or other tree decoration and a cracker inside it
- Photocopy the activity sheets you want to use and do any cutting out for the younger children. Complete a clock

Depending on your choice of activities, you may need:
- postcards and stamps
- split-pin paper fasteners
- cotton wool, doilies and ribbon
- a Christmas catalogue with Christmas cards in it

## Five weeks to go – Introducing the theme of the play

The aim this week is to read the story of the play to the children, to give them a taste of a Victorian Christmas and to bring home the real meaning of Christmas amidst all the elaborate preparations.

Ask the children about all the things that they or their families are busy doing before Christmas. Gradually bring out your visual aids to prompt the children. For example, ask, *Do you have any shopping to do? What do you need to buy? … Do you help with any cooking? … Do you send anything through the post? …*

*Do you decorate your home? ...*

Tell them that you have done a little Christmas shopping already! Bring out the cracker and pull it with one of the children. Put on the paper hat and read out the joke. Mention that crackers used to be just a bag of sweets which two children could pull apart, but that in 1860, when Queen Victoria was on the throne, an English firm added a snap to make the bang when the cracker came apart.

Explain that you are going to tell them a story about some Victorian children who saw something amazing happen in their own village one Christmas Eve when everyone was busy getting ready for Christmas Day. Read '*Shine your lights!*' making sure that the children see all the pictures.

# Shine your lights!

'I do love Christmas Eve,' said Daisy, warming her toes in front of the fire. 'Holly round the fireplace...'

'A huge dish of cook's mince pies...' added William, his cheeks bulging.

'Stockings waiting to be filled...' sighed Bella.

'And don't forget baby Jesus, born in a stable,' said Edward. He peered out of the cottage window.

'Perhaps Mary and Joseph are out there now, looking for somewhere to stay.'

'Don't be silly!' cried William. 'That all happened a long time ago.'

A tabby cat sprang on to the window-sill, mewing loudly.

'You are restless!' laughed Edward. 'What are you trying to tell me?' He gathered the furry bundle to his chest and opened the front door.

'Out you go ... shoo! And don't go chasing the poor ducks. Their pond is frozen solid tonight.'

Puss scampered away, frightened by the excited voices of a band of children coming along the street.

'Come and join us!' they called.

'Bring a lantern and bring a shawl. Tomorrow is Christmas and snow may fall!'

'Carol singers!' exclaimed Edward. 'If we hurry, we can catch them up!'

They made their way to the village green, stopping here and there to sing

# cOUNTDOWN TO THE PLAY DAY!

Christmas carols. Cooks busy making pastry looked up from basement windows to wave their floury hands. Lords and ladies danced at the manor house, and the children at the rectory left their Christmas tree and came running to the window. Away from the cosy cottages, coldness gripped the village green. Icicles glistened on the bare branches of a tree, and a freezing mist hung on the fields. The singers blew hot air on their hands and stamped their feet to keep warm.

Huddled together like the snowy white

ducks, the four children sang carol after carol, until they felt quite dizzy with tiredness and the cold. At last, the church clock chimed its thin notes and the other singers drifted away.

'What *is* the time?' yawned Bella.

Edward looked up at the old clock face. 'That's strange!' he said. 'I can't tell. Look at the hands on the clock. They're spinning round! Faster and faster!'

The children stared at the clock in amazement, blinking their tired eyes.

'Let's go,' said Daisy nervously. 'It must be very late.'

'Hang on a minute,' said William. 'I want to see what happens. Look! The hands are slowing down now. There! It's stopped on midnight!'

'Perhaps time has stopped,' whispered Bella. 'Perhaps the world is waiting for something tremendous to happen.'

'Meow,' agreed a tabby cat.

'It's Puss!' cried Daisy. She ran towards her, but stopped as two figures appeared, as if from nowhere, limping towards them out of the mist.

'Who's that?' asked William. 'I don't know

them at all. What strange clothes!'

The couple, a man and a woman, knocked at the first cottage door, which opened and then shut again quickly. The same thing happened at the second cottage, the third and the fourth, and at the manor house they saw the manservant shake his head gravely.

'No room for guests!' breathed Edward. 'No room on Christmas Eve!'

'You don't mean ... it *can't* be Mary and Joseph,' exclaimed Bella, staring at the couple as they approached the inn.

'But if it is,' said Daisy, 'the innkeeper will let them have his stable. He's bound to!'

'You're right!' said Edward. 'Quick, shine your lights up into the porch!'

They held their breath as the innkeeper came outside, wiping his hands on his apron. His kind face filled with pity at the sight of the exhausted travellers and he nodded and beckoned.

'Hurrah!' chorused the children. 'There's room at our own village inn!'

'Perhaps we should go home now,' said Edward. 'There's nothing more we can do!'

'Except see baby Jesus!' Daisy retorted. 'Really Edward, we can't go home now!

Besides, time seems to have stopped!'

The children waited, no longer feeling cold. They watched the first flakes of snow float down, brushing their cheeks and noses and dusting the ground like the white icing on Cook's Christmas cake.

'Should we ... do you think we dare peep in the stable now?' asked Daisy.

They crunched through the snow, Puss boldly leading the way.

'Girls first!' whispered William.

'No, after you!' said Bella and Daisy together.

'Don't be shy!' said a deep voice. Joseph

stood smiling at them from the doorway.
'Come and see the baby. You're our first
visitors.'

Jesus lay in the manger, as they knew he
would.

'Is it all right if we …'

'Of course!' said Mary. 'Come as close as
you like. You can even hold his hand.'

The children fell on their knees in the
straw.

'Oh, he's lovely,' gasped Bella.

'Look at his tiny hands,' said Daisy.

'He's looking straight at us,' said Edward
delightedly, 'as if he knows us already!'

William said nothing, but his eyes shone
with delight.

It was a while before the children noticed
a familiar sound—the gentle purring of a
contented cat!

'Look at Puss on Mary's lap!' said William,
finding his voice at last. 'And look at all the
other animals, kneeling down in the
straw!'

'So this is your cat,' said Mary. 'He's
keeping me nice and warm. Can I borrow
him for the night?'

'I think we ought to be going now,' said
Edward. 'Just in case you have any more
visitors.'

'I don't want to leave all this,' sighed Bella.
'You were right, Edward. This is what
Christmas is all about!'

'Goodbye, baby Jesus,' said Daisy, dragging
herself away. 'We'll never forget you.
Never!'

The children stepped out into thick snow.
Stars twinkled in the clear sky. Sweet music
seemed to come from the surrounding
hills, rolling down the steep slopes and
filling the air.

'Whatever's that?' asked Bella. 'It sounds
like bells ringing in another village.'

'Those are angel voices,' said Edward wisely. 'Can you see their glowing lights on the hillside?'

'And what are those dark shapes leaping and coming towards us?' asked William.

'Those must be the shepherds,' cried Daisy triumphantly. 'Let's shine our lights again and guide them to the stable.'

The children held up their flickering lanterns and the shepherds, breathless from the long trudge through the snow, followed the dancing beams towards the stable and in at the open door.

The children left the shelter of the inn and walked dreamily around the green and into the street that led back home. The ancient roofs that overhung the street had kept off most of the snow but the uneven cobbles glittered with frost. The clatter of hooves interrupted their thoughts.

'What a din!' said William, holding his ears. 'I thought I saw all the horses in the stable.'

'I wonder,' muttered Edward. 'Horses, or camels, do you think?'

The children gasped as large shadows fell across the street, lurching backwards and forwards in a slow, steady rhythm. And suddenly, there were those Eastern kings, brilliant in rich colours and exotic patterns.

'Stand back!' ordered Edward as the camels strode past them, decked in thick braids and tassels.

'Can you believe that!' William whistled. 'Those camels were enormous!'

'They had golden saddles!' cried Bella. 'But I didn't have time to see any precious gifts.'

'We could go back to the stable,' suggested Daisy, eagerly. 'Just one glimpse of them all. What do you say, Edward?'

But Edward was gazing sadly at the church clock.

'I'm afraid there wouldn't be much point,' he said. 'Look, the hands are moving on again.' And as if to confirm it, the clock struck midnight, loud and long!

'The angel music has stopped,' said Bella. 'And their glowing lights have disappeared. Oh, Edward, it wasn't a dream, was it?'

'No,' he replied, 'I'm sure it was true!'

'I do love Christmas Day,' said Daisy, as they opened their stockings the next morning. 'Jesus is born! Let's go to church to say thank you!'

'I'll wear my new hat to celebrate!' said Bella.

'And I'll wear my new scarf!' said William. 'What's in your stocking, Edward?'

Before he could answer, there was a dreadful scratching and scrabbling at the front door.

'It's Puss!' yelled Edward, running to let her in. 'You dear, dear cat. You knew all along where you were going last night, didn't you!'

Along the street, voices called 'Happy Christmas' and the church bells rang out, joyful and festive.

'What a shame!' said Daisy. 'Now it's too late for the villagers to see baby Jesus in the manger.'

The children hurried to church and entered by the heavy wooden door. The carol singers stood in a group, whispering excitedly.

'Come and look at this!' they cried.

'Come and see Jesus in the manger.'

Puzzled, the children went closer. A beautiful nativity set, delicately carved in wood, lay on the old flagstones. There were the shepherds with their lambs, and there were the kings offering their rich gifts. Mary and Joseph smiled down at the tiny baby.

'How lovely,' said Daisy. 'Now everyone can see what we saw!'

'I wish *we'd* given the baby something,' said Bella. 'We didn't think of that.'

'We gave him the best present of all,' said Edward. 'Our loving hearts.'

'It's a perfect nativity scene, isn't it?' cried Daisy. 'Nothing's missing ...'

'Except for one thing!' said Edward mysteriously, pulling a tiny china cat out of his pocket. 'I found this in my stocking this morning, but I think it belongs just here.' And he placed the cat down in the straw, beside the wooden animals.

'Oh, Edward!' laughed the others.

# Activity time

Divide the children into groups according to which activity you want them to do.

## The Christmas crackers

Use the pictures on the three Christmas cards to talk to the children about a typical Victorian Christmas. You could say that the Christmas tree was a German idea, and that when Prince Albert married Queen Victoria in 1840, he brought the idea with him.

Ask the children if they have ever been carol singing and whether they collected money for charity. See how many traditional carols the children can name. Did they know that the original music to 'Silent Night' was written for two voices and a guitar because the church mice had damaged the organ and it was awaiting repair?

Look at the robin acting as a postman. When the penny post was introduced in 1840, the postmen wore red uniforms and were sometimes referred to as 'Robin postmen'.

Which card do they think has most to do with the real meaning of Christmas?

When they have coloured in their favourite card, the children can glue it on to a postcard and send it to a friend. They could even have a go at writing a rhyming greeting. Alternatively, make a display for the play day. The Victorians put their cards in albums.

## Snowflakes

Show your own completed clock, and use the hands to point to the pictures as you briefly retell the story of the play. When they have coloured the pictures, help them to attach the hands, pre-cut for a younger group. Older children can do this themselves, and use the clock as a reminder to write the story in their own words, perhaps from the point of view of the cat.

## Robins

Help the children to make Victorian-style angels and use them as props in the play. If you have done the cutting out, very young children can manage to stick on the materials.

## Further ideas

### Christmas card game

Bring in a catalogue of Christmas cards and look at them with the children. How many of them show baby Jesus or a nativity scene? You could make a chart and stick the pictures of the cards in two columns to show which are to do with the real meaning of Christmas and which are not. Work out the percentage. In Victorian times, very few cards were religious and the popular themes were holly, mistletoe, plum pudding, Father Christmas, Christmas trees, bells and robins.

## Closing prayer

*Thank you, God, for all the fun we will have*
   *this Christmas*
   *writing our cards and making mince pies,*
   *singing carols and decorating the tree.*
*When we are busy, don't let us forget*
   *the reason for all the celebrations—*
   *baby Jesus who was born in a stable.*
**Amen**

## Memos for next week

- Read 'Four weeks to go'
- Read the play again and study the starting position and stage directions for all the children
- Make sure you have the essential props ready to use straight away. (Try to set up the stage before the children arrive.)
- If possible, take a music stand to put the play on while you are directing the action
- Take a large pair of men's shoes!
- Photocopy the activity sheets from pages 87 to 91, so that each child has the one that features his or her character
- Take materials for the collage if you decide to make it

## Four weeks to go – Introducing the characters

The aim this week is to encourage the children to step into the characters' shoes, to become part of the story and to take the first steps towards turning it into a play.

Hold up the large pair of shoes. Ask someone small to come and try them on and stomp about in them. Explain what it *really* means to put yourself in someone else's shoes—to see things through their eyes and to feel what they feel.

Remind the children of the story you told them last week. Ask them to imagine that they are one of the four children as you read the paragraph below. They should close their eyes and picture everything in their minds as you read slowly, pausing often.

You are sitting by a roaring fire, eating a delicious tea. Can you hear the wood crackling … can you smell the burning logs and feel the heat on your face? But what's that? It sounds like singing coming from outside. It's getting louder … and louder … yes, it's some carol singers.

You want to go and join in with the fun. Quick, where are your warm clothes? You open the door and run out into the cold night. Can you feel the freezing air on your cheek? Can you smell snow in the air? Can you see the ducks huddled up at the side of their frozen pond? You're glad to see the glowing lanterns of the carol singers and you hurry to catch them up. Careful, don't slip—the path is very icy.

As you sing, you can see your breath, like a wispy cloud floating away on the night air—floating away to join the mist hanging on the fields. The church steeple seems to rise up out of the mist, like the mast of a ghostly ship, and suddenly you feel a little dizzy. Is it your imagination, or did you see the hands on the church clock spinning? And is it your imagination, or did you see two strange figures walking towards you, through the first flakes of snow?

Ask everyone to open their eyes again. Get the children to finish the story by asking them questions. For example, *Does anyone know who the two people were? ... What were they looking for? ... Did all the busy people in the houses invite them in? ... etc ... What was the first thing the children thought about on Christmas Day?*

Tell everyone who they are going to be in the play and remind them to try to put themselves into that character's shoes. Read the play to the children or ask them to read it aloud from photocopied scripts.

# Activity time

Use the activity sheets in whichever way you like, to help the children learn their parts. (Let the children suggest their own ideas about the acting so that the play becomes their own.) You may like to divide up into four groups to begin with, as follows: the **carol singers**, to include the four children and the cat; the **villagers**, to include the cooks, the lords and ladies, and the mother and children; the **nativity characters**, to include the church clock; and the **narrators**.

## The carol singers

If you want each of the four children to have a line, you could divide the verse at the top of the Carol Singers activity sheet (page 87) between them and mark up a master copy of the play. (This verse is spoken by Narrator 4 in the original.) The children could choose Victorian names for themselves.

The carol singers can practise the song to the tune of 'Girls and boys come out to play' and see if they can march round at the same time as singing it. Read on in the play as far as 'It's freezing cold tonight', so that the children can work on letting the cat out, and Edward can practise leading the other three to join the carol party.

## The villagers

The villagers have less to practise, so they could spend some time colouring in the activity sheets and making the Victorian house with its opening windows. Get the children to mime their parts as you read out their lines and then see if they can mime while speaking the lines themselves. Work on getting their actions to fit in with the rhythm of the words.

## The church clock, the innkeeper and the nativity characters

Start to read the play from the line, 'The church clock strikes the hour. Listen!' and decide whether the child playing the clock will be responsible for sounding a gong or whether this will be done off stage. Practise the arm movements for the hands of the clock.

## A crowd of angels sing with joy

Read on, asking the children to listen out for the cue to their own line. The shepherds need to jump up quickly and, like the angels, practise speaking as one, and the kings have to name their particular gift as they place it on the floor.

## The narrators

Give each of them their own copy of the play and ask them to practise reading their verses to each other, slowly and with lots of expression. Ask them to imagine what the characters on the stage will be doing so that they pause long enough to allow for this. They can help each other and make constructive comments.

# Further ideas

Make a collage of the village in the play with its church, village green, duck pond, cottages, inn and stable. Position the various buildings so that they correspond with the layout on stage.

# It's play time!

Move to the stage area which you have already set up and ask everyone to sit in the appropriate place for the start of the play. (See stage plan on page 95.) Let the children imagine the layout of the village, by saying, *This is where the children live, over on this side; this is the village green at the front here; this is the old inn with the stable, etc.*

Now start the play in earnest and try to link the sections you have practised in your groups. Everyone should be still for the first three verses, with the four children coming to life in verse four. Make sure that your narrators are leaving enough time for all the mimes and a suitable pause between verses. Remind them to read slowly and clearly.

Give lots of encouragement and praise and lead the children in the mimes marked 'all'.

Don't worry too much about the archway this week. The activities for next time will give the children some practice at this.

You may wish to sing any carols the children already know at the appropriate moments, or leave this to a later rehearsal.

If you don't have time for the whole play, make a note to start next week at the point where you left off.

## Closing prayer

*Thank you, God, for the kind innkeeper*
*    who felt sorry for Mary and Joseph out in the cold.*
*Please help us to understand*
*    how other people are feeling*
*    and to put ourselves in their shoes.*
***Amen***

## Memos for next week

- Read 'Three weeks to go'
- Provide some playing cards and board games
- You will need music for 'Lighting the porches' and 'Musical statues'
- You will need a shoebox, yellow tissue paper and a torch for each nativity scene

## Three weeks to go – Let's play parlour games

This week, have fun playing some games which contain ideas and actions similar to those in the play. You may like to let the children have a short time playing board or card games.

Explain that the Victorians had no televisions or computers and so they amused themselves with games, songs around the piano and dancing. You could ask the children about their favourite games and whether they like to play anything special with their families at Christmas.

### Lighting the porches

Ask three or four children to choose a partner. The pairs should stand facing one another so that they form two lines, holding hands along the lines, next to your innkeeper at one end, and some distance from Mary and Joseph at the other.

Play some dance music as the children gallop for eight beats towards Mary and Joseph, and eight beats back again. (Everyone else can clap to the music.) The dancers quickly raise

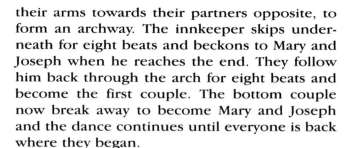

their arms towards their partners opposite, to form an archway. The innkeeper skips underneath for eight beats and beckons to Mary and Joseph when he reaches the end. They follow him back through the arch for eight beats and become the first couple. The bottom couple now break away to become Mary and Joseph and the dance continues until everyone is back where they began.

Make sure that the carol singers have a turn at this as it will help them to form an archway quickly in the play.

### Musical statues

Ask the children to dance to some lively music. When the music stops, they must freeze like statues. Anyone who moves is out. Keep going until you have a winner. Remind the children that the nativity characters represent a nativity set at the end of the play and that they must keep very still. If you have a set, you could let the children put it together at this point, ready to display on the play day.

### Charades

Divide into two teams and give pairs of children a mime to act out to their own team. Let each pair have a few moments to work out how they are going to do it and ask the team not to make any guesses until the actors have finished. Try to include any ideas linked with the mimes in the play, for example:

- roll up your sleeves and make some pastry
- light a candle in a lantern
- call in the cat and feed him
- change a baby's nappy and put him into his cot
- put the angel on the top of your Christmas tree
- saddle up a horse and go for a ride

Give a point for every correct guess and see which is the winning team.

## Activity time

The children could make a nativity scene in a shoebox, either individually or in groups, and pretend that they are the carol singers peeping into the stable. Instructions are on page 89.

Cut a hole in the lid and cover with yellow tissue paper. Then 'shine your lights' into the hole and peep in through the stable door.

## It's play time!

You may wish to rehearse in your four groups again before joining together.

If you didn't manage to get to the end of the play last time, start where you left off and work on the nativity characters and the nativity scene at the end. Get everyone to decide what pose they will adopt and to practise keeping still.

## Closing prayer

*Father God, we thank you for Christmas time,*
*and the opportunity to celebrate with our families.*
*This Christmas, help us to remember to keep still for*
*a moment, just as we did in the play,*
*and to think about the birth of Jesus.*
**Amen**

## Memos for next week

- Read 'Two weeks to go'
- Take any pictures you can find of Victorian costume and costume designs for theatre productions
- Photocopy the activity sheet on dressing up from page 93
- Decide which costumes and props to make and take the appropriate craft materials
- Locate a gong, coconut halves and bells for the sound effects

## Two weeks to go – Costumes and props

Leave more time this week for practising the play.

It is up to you to decide how elaborate or simple the costumes are to be. This section gives some ideas about involving the children in planning what they will wear.

Look at pictures of Victorian costume in books, whether fiction or non-fiction, with the children. Ask them to keep a look-out for Victorian pictures on Christmas cards or biscuit tins. Talk about the clothes and point out the distinctive features, such as the girls' bows and sashes and the boys' gaiters and buckle shoes.

Explain the role of a costume designer in a theatre and show any pictures you may have in theatre programmes or books of the designs for the costumes. Ask the children to think what they could find at home (or make) to wear for their part in the play.

## Activity time

Give the children the 'Design-a-costume' sheet (page 93) and ask them to design their own costume in the same way, with a few notes to explain each item. They could colour the designs and display them on the wall.

## Further ideas

### Clock costume

Paint or colour two rectangular pieces of card in greys and browns for the church tower. Glue a clock face on each, either drawing your own or using the one on page 85. Punch holes in the top and sides and attach the tabard over the shoulders and around the waist with black shoelaces.

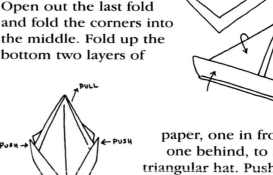

### Steeple hat

Fold a rectangular piece of brown paper (about A2 size) in half and half again. Open out the last fold and fold the corners into the middle. Fold up the bottom two layers of paper, one in front and one behind, to make a triangular hat. Push in the sides to make a steeple shape and staple so that it fits the head snugly. Keep in place with hair grips or elastic.

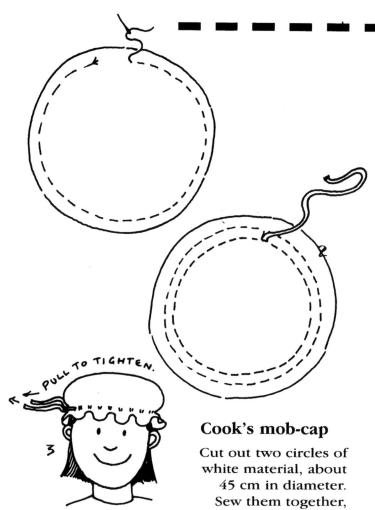

## Paper lanterns

Fold a rectangular piece of coloured paper in half lengthways and make regular cuts along the folded edge. Open it out and glue the two ends together to make a lantern. Cut a strip of paper and attach as a handle.

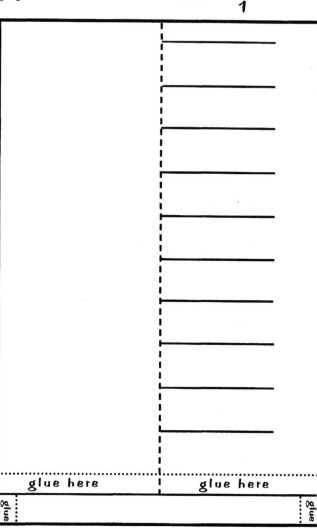

## Cook's mob-cap

Cut out two circles of white material, about 45 cm in diameter. Sew them together, leaving a gap of several centimetres. Turn the cap inside out. Oversew the gap, and press flat. Make a double row of stitching about 5 cm from the edge, leaving room between the two rows for your elastic. Make a small cut between the rows (on the inside of the cap) and thread the elastic (attached to a small safety-pin) around the cap. Pull up to the correct size and knot the elastic.

Alternatively, buy a lacy bath cap.

## Christmas cat

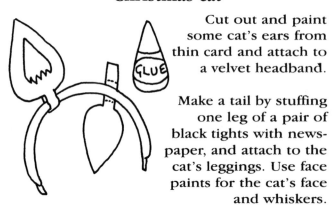

Cut out and paint some cat's ears from thin card and attach to a velvet headband.

Make a tail by stuffing one leg of a pair of black tights with newspaper, and attach to the cat's leggings. Use face paints for the cat's face and whiskers.

## Girls' bows and ladies' flowers

Make some bows and flowers out of coloured crêpe or tissue paper and attach to dresses, shoes and hair.

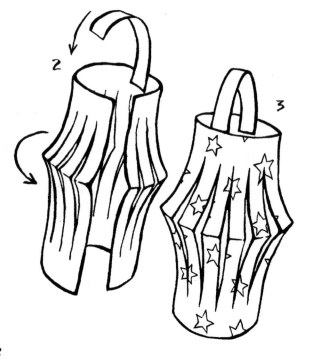

## It's play time!

Try to go through the entire play this week, singing all the carols at the appropriate moments. It's important that the children see the play as a complete story now rather than in confusing bits and pieces.

Remind them to really act their parts, especially showing the wonder of the carol singers at seeing the baby born in their own village stable. You could ask them where they think Mary and Joseph would find shelter in your village or town.

Try to make the ending as joyful as possible and ensure the last line is spoken with great confidence.

Decide who will do the sound effects for you.

## Closing prayer

*Thank you, God, for all the fun we have had*
*thinking about our costumes for the play.*
*Help us to remember that whatever we look like*
*on the outside, you can see what we are*
*really like on the inside.*
*Please give us kind and loving hearts.*
**Amen**

## Memos for next week

- Read 'One week to go'
- Take a completed shoebox nativity and a torch
- Photocopy the poster
- Make sure that all your arrangements are in place for the day of the play, including any plans you have for refreshments afterwards
- Ask the children to bring in their costumes if you want a dress rehearsal

# One week to go – come to our play!

This week, be determined to leave as much time as you need to rehearse the play without letting other activities overrun. You may wish to invite another class to watch the rehearsal as this will get everyone used to an audience.

Warn the narrators to be sensitive to the reaction of the audience, and to pause if they laugh or clap unexpectedly!

If you made the shoebox nativity last week, hold it away from any light sources and ask several children to see if they can make out the figures inside. Now shine a torch in the top, and ask them if this is any better. Explain that their play is really trying to 'shine a light' on the real meaning of Christmas for the audience.

## Activity time

Ask everyone to colour in the posters for the play and put some around the school or in your church. Let the children take one home. Use the 'Please bring…' section as appropriate, for example, *mince pies, friends and relatives,* or *Sam dressed in his costume*!

## It's play time!

Decide how the children will get into their starting positions. If you want everyone to lead on in an orderly line, work out the correct order and practise walking into position several times. Ask the children to remember who is in front of them, and who is behind in the line.

If this is a dress rehearsal, take the opportunity to iron out any problems with costumes or props. Discard a prop rather than letting it interfere with the play.

Remind the narrators to read slowly and with lots of expression and to make sure they are allowing enough time for the action on stage.

Be as encouraging as you can and give lots of praise so that the children feel confident and excited about the play day.

## Closing prayer

*Thank you, Lord Jesus, for helping us*
*with our play today.*
*We pray that everything will go well on the play day*
*so that we can shine a light*
*on the real meaning of Christmas.*
**Amen**

## Memos for the play day

- Read 'It's the play day!'
- Take any 'thank you' presents or cards for your helpers

# \* It's the play day! \*

Join in with the children's excitement and make today special.

It's essential to let the children 'warm up' before they go out to perform, so sing some carols and chant the last line of the play several times. Remind everyone to speak up loudly and clearly so that even those in the back row can hear.

Be prepared to give any necessary prompts quickly and loudly during the play. This will be far less disconcerting than a big silence. Impress upon the children that the hard work is all over. Now all they need to do is to go out and enjoy themselves!

Check that the stage is properly set up and that the baby doll is hidden in the manger.

# It's time, everybody!

- Make sure that the children have all been to the toilet.

Just before you lead on to the stage, you may like to say this prayer:

## A prayer for our play

*Father God, please bless our nativity play.*
*Give us smiling faces and big voices*
    *so that everyone will be able to enjoy our story.*
*We pray that Jesus will be born in our hearts*
    *this Christmas.*
**Amen**

On you go! Shine those lights ...
and **enjoy yourselves!**

# Shine Your LIGHTS!

## by Vicki Howie

**Narr 1:** We don't know how it happened.
We really cannot say.
We *do* know that we saw the baby,
Lying in the hay.

**Narr 2:** Some said it must have been a dream.
But we know what we saw.
We shone our lights, and beams danced in
The open stable door.

**Narr 3:** The year was 1878,
The best night—Christmas Eve!
An icy one, the village pond
Was frozen, I believe.

**Narr 4:** The four of us were eating supper,
Tasting Cook's delicious pie,
When Edward heard the Christmas music—

**Edward:** Carol singers going by!

**CAROL: Girls and boys come out to sing**

**The singers process around the stage, finishing centre front.**

**Narr 1:** Then it was, Eat up your supper …
*(All mime eating, 'yum, yum')*
Put out the cat …
*(The four children shoo the cat out, and the cat joins the innkeeper)*
Tie on your brightest scarf …
*(All mime tying scarf)*
Pull on your warmest hat …
*(All mime pulling on hat)*
And follow me to the village green
*(Edward beckons and leads on)*
Sing carols round my light …
*(The four children join singers)*
Rub your hands …
*(All rub hands)*
Stamp your feet …
*(All stamp feet)*
It's freezing cold tonight!

**Narr 2:** We sang our Christmas songs to people, busy as could be.
If you peep inside bright windows, you'll see …

**Cooks:** Cooks are rolling pastry …
*(Cooks/all mime rolling pastry)*

**L and L:** Lords and ladies dance …
*(Lords and Ladies/all curtsy or bow)*

**Mother:** And mother helps the children
Hang an angel on each branch
*(Mother helps children, and angels raise arms above heads)*

**CAROL: O Christmas tree, O Christmas tree**

**Narr 3:** The church clock strikes the hour. Listen!
*(All cup ears, and gong sounds)*
Mist hangs on the fields, icicles glisten…
*(All wiggle fingers)*
And as we look up at the old village clock,
The hands circle madly … then slow down … then stop!
*(Clock/all circle arms and singers stand back, near manger, to reveal Mary and Joseph entering at back)*

**Narr 4:** And who is this man and his wife in a shawl,
Stumbling along as the snow starts to fall?
*(They approach the villagers)*
Knocking on doors for a warm place to rest …
*(All mime knocking)*
But the answer that echoes is…

**All:** No room for guests!
*(As if calling out of windows)*

**Mary:** Joseph, the night's getting colder and colder.

**Joseph:** We'll find somewhere soon, Mary. Lean on my shoulder.

**Narr 1:** Now shine your lights, shine your torches …
*(Singers swing lanterns)*
Light the doorways, light the porches…
*(Singers form archway)*
Here comes the innkeeper nodding his head …
*(Innkeeper comes through arch)*

**Inn:** Yes! You can have the horse's shed!
*(He beckons)*

**All:** Hurrah!

**Innkeeper takes Mary and Joseph through arch to the chairs and they sit down. The singers kneel down.**

**Narr 2:** Should we… dare we… peep in at the door,
Where horses and donkeys kneel down in the straw?
*(Singers remain kneeling but peer into stable)*
For here in the warmth and safe from all danger,
Jesus is born …
*(Mary picks up doll from manger and rocks)*
And sleeps in the manger.
*(Mary gently replaces doll)*

**All:** SSSHH!!

**CAROL: Run with torches to light the dim stable**

**Narr 3:** We hate to go and leave all that …
Why, Mary even stroked our cat! …
*(Mary strokes cat, and all meow)*
And step outside where snow lies deep…
*(Singers go to sit on back box)*
And songs float down from the hillside steep
*(Angels stand up)*
A crowd of angels sing with joy…

**Angels:** Come, shepherds, find the baby boy!

**CAROL: Andrew mine, Jasper mine**

**Narr 4:** The shepherds jump up, as if to say…

**Sheps:** Let's find that baby straight away!

**Narr 4:** And so we point towards the stable,
Tucked beneath the old inn's gable.
*(Shepherds follow directions to stable)*
We shine our lights until we're sure
They've found the open stable door!
*(Shepherds kneel at manger)*

**Narr 1:** But listen!
*(Singers cup ears)*

The distant clatter of hooves
Rings out on the pavement beneath ancient roofs …
*(Make clip-clop sound)*
And wise men, dressed in patterns bold,
Come riding on camels whose saddles are gold…
*(Wise men ride to manger)*
These Eastern kings kneel down in the straw …
*(They kneel beside manger)*
And lay precious gifts on the stony floor …

**King 1:** Gold!

**King 2:** Frankincense!

**King 3:** Myrrh!

**All:** Ahh!

**Narr 2:** But wait! The hands of the clock move on …
*(Clock walks stiffly to stand by nativity scene/all circle arms again)*
And we hear it strike midnight loud and long …
*(Gong sounds, then fades)*
The angels disappear from view …
*(Angels fly to stand behind nativity scene)*
Was it a dream?

**Singers:** *(loudly to audience)* NO! I'M SURE IT WAS TRUE!

**The four children wave goodnight to their friends and go back to their stools.**

**Narr 3:** We don't know how it happened.
We really cannot say.
We only know we loved that baby,
When we woke on Christmas Day!
*(All yawn and stretch)*

**CAROL:** *(softly at first, then louder)*
**We wish you a merry Christmas**

**Singers process around the stage again, finishing centre front.**

**Narr 4:** Then it was, Finish your breakfast …
*(All mime eating, 'yum, yum')*
Call in the cat …
*(The four children entice cat, 'Here Puss', who joins them)*
Tie on your new scarf …
*(All mime tying scarf)*
Pull on your new hat …
*(All mime pulling on hat)*
And follow me to the village green,
All those in windows bright …
*(Edward beckons to the villagers, and everyone joins singers at front)*
It's not too late to kneel before the baby born last night!

**Narr 1:** Listen! Church bells ring out joy and festivity!
*(Bells ring off stage)*
Look! Through the church door, a tiny nativity!
*(Singers point at nativity characters, who keep very still)*
Hurry! Let's kneel by the babe in the hay …
*(Singers and villagers kneel)*
For Jesus is born in our hearts today!

**All:** *(joyfully)* Yes! Jesus is born in our hearts today!

## THE END

# Shine Your Lights! 5 weeks to go

## Christmas crackers Activity sheet

# Post early for Christmas!

Which is your favourite card? Colour it, add a rhyme, glue to a postcard and send.

*'A kindly word and a cheery rhyme
To wish you a happy Christmas time.'*

Snowflakes
Activity sheet

Time for a story!

Cut out the hands and fix to the clock
with a split-pin paper fastener.

## Robins Activity sheet
# An angel for your tree!

1. Colour your angel.

2. Cut out small wedge-shaped pieces from a doily and glue to her ruff.

3. Glue strands of cotton wool to her wings.
   (Pull off any big lumps to leave a feathery effect.)

4. Cut round your angel and attach a loop of ribbon to the back of her head.

5. Now hang the angel on a
   branch of your tree.

### Activity sheet

# The carol singers

The four of us were eating supper,
Tasting Cook's delicious pie,
When Edward heard the Christmas music…

*'Carol singers going by!'*

*Girls and boys come out to sing,*

*We'll make the bells in the steeple ring,*

*Leave your supper and leave your sleep,*

*Come join your playfellows in the street.*

*Come with a whoop and come with a call,*

*Come with a good will or not at all.*

*Bring a lantern and bring a shawl,*

*Tomorrow is Christmas and snow may fall!*

PUT THE CAT OUT SHOO!

# The villagers

We sang our Christmas songs to people, busy as could be.
If you peep inside bright windows, you'll see ...

Lords and ladies dance!

the children hang an angel on each branch!
And mother helps

Cooks are rolling pastry!

Cut out the house shape.
Cut along the dotted lines to open the windows.
Paste to 'The villagers' activity sheet.

# The church clock, the innkeeper and the nativity characters

And as we look up at the old village clock,
The hands circle madly … then slow down … then stop!

A crowd of angels sing with joy . . .

Come, shepherds, find the baby boy!

The shepherds jump up, as if to say . . .

Let's find that baby straight away!

These Eastern kings kneel down in the straw . . .
And lay precious gifts on the stony floor . . .

Frankincense!

Gold!

Myrrh!

Activity sheet

**A**

Colour and glue to the inside end of a shoebox

**B**

Colour and glue several inches in front of A

Fold and glue to side

Fold and glue to side

Colour and glue in front of B

Colour and glue in front of B

Should we, dare we peep in at the door?

Colour door and glue to outside end. Cut around top section to view nativity.

Fold and glue to base.

Fold and glue to base

92

## Activity sheet
# Design-a-costume!

Design a costume for the character you are going to be in the play.

make a paper lantern

holly

borrow Dad's cap if he says 'yes'

my red scarf

school blazer

thick trousers tucked into socks

black lace-ups, tape gold buckle or curtain ring to top

**Boy carol singer**

put holly in headband

tie hair back with ribbon

blue mittens

old straw hat

white school shirt

borrow Mum's shawl if she will let me

this is my pinafore dress (it's quite long)

red tights

black boots

**Girl carol singer**

93

# Shine Your LIGHTS!

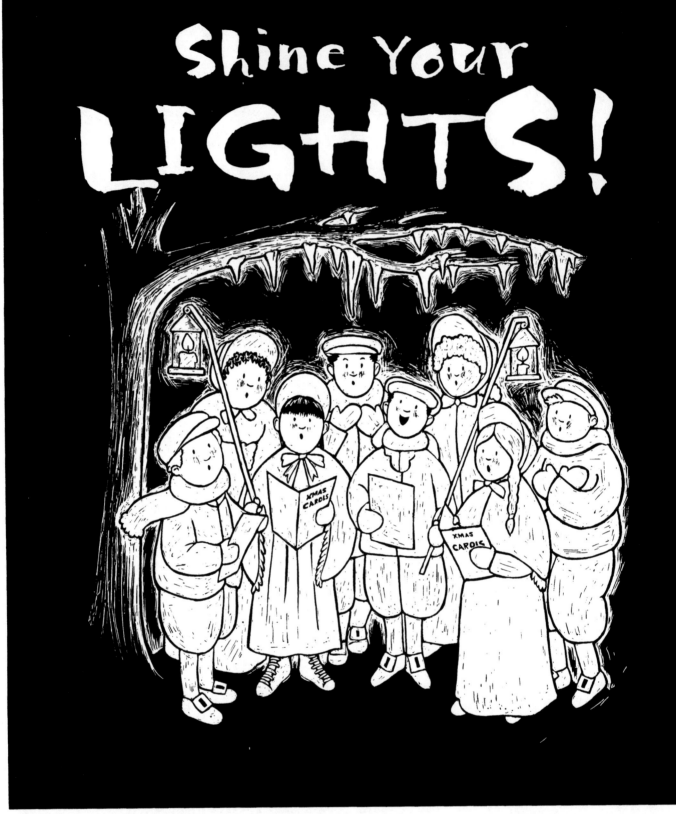

A nativity play performed by: _____

on: _____ at: _____

place: _____

Please bring: _____

We don't know how it happened . . .

A crowd of angels sing with joy . . .

Yes! Jesus is born in our hearts today!

Printed in the United Kingdom
by Lightning Source UK Ltd.
115401UKS00001B/63-336